Advance Praise for *Jan's Story*

"*Jan's Story* is about never forgetting what we once had cherished… what we once had and lost."
~ **Katie Couric,** Anchor-Managing Editor, CBS Evening News

"This is a love story, a travelogue, a television history…and a stunning, achingly personal journey. Dashing and fearless, nothing could stop Barry, the veteran war correspondent, until tragedy knocked him cold. This is the story of life, love, loss and renewal."
~ **Brian Williams,** Anchor-Managing Editor, NBC Nightly News

"An intimate and courageously honest memoir about devastating loss, enduring love, and finding the strength to carry on, *Jan's Story* is a gift to other families dealing with younger onset Alzheimer's, not because their challenges and decisions will exactly mirror Barry's and Jan's, but because they will know that they're not alone."
~ **Lisa Genova,** New York Times bestselling author of *Still Alice*

"I knew my long time CBS News colleague Barry Petersen, one of the best and most admired correspondents in the business, through his unforgettable coverage of important events in faraway places all over the world. In *Jan's Story* he uses all his writing and reporting skills to tell the story of what happened to shatter his own world. Now I understand better how vulnerable we all are to the most terrible kind of identity theft."
~ **Charles Osgood,** Anchor, CBS News Sunday Morning

"No one who has ever been a caregiver, ever questions when another says, "I can't do it anymore." *Jan's Story* is a must read by every caregiver, family member and well meaning friends."
~ **Meryl Comer,** President, Geoffrey Beene Foundation, Alzheimer's Initiative

"Have the courage to read this book with an open heart and mind, talk about it, and interrupt the silence."
~ **Lisa Snyder, MSW, LCSW,** Dir, Quality of Life Programs, UC-San Diego Shiley-Marcos Alzheimer's Disease Research Ctr., author of *Speaking Our Minds – What it's Like to Have Alzheimer's.*

"Barry Petersen's utterly honest love story moved me to tears. With a reporter's eye for detail and a poet's insight, he poignantly shares his desperate attempt to care for the wife he adores. The book succeeds because he hides nothing."
~ **Jon LaPook, MD** - Medical Correspondent, CBS Evening News with Katie Couric, Associate Clinical Professor of Medicine-Columbia University Medical Center

"I knew Jan and Barry from their days in Moscow, London and Asia. She was intelligent, talented, and gracious, always with a smile and with a wonderful sense of humor...as true as the blue of a Texas sky. Barry and Jan were slowly, excruciatingly lowered into a version of hell ...and faced heartbreak with courage and Alzheimer's Disease with a will to survive."
~ **Dan Rather,** Anchor, Dan Rather Reports, HDNet

"This story of immense love and the terrible loneliness of caregiving left me in tears. As Jan surrendered to the ravages of Alzheimer's, Barry cared for her as best he could. I know firsthand the demands of caregiving. When I was 12 years old, my father became terminally ill with leukemia. As the oldest and as a daughter, I helped my 34 year old mother. Caregivers like Barry often feel isolated, inadequate, and not knowing where to turn for help or how to share their feelings of despair with others. As America ages, many more of us will become caregivers, and millions will soon be making the same journey that Barry made with his beloved Jan. This book will give comfort to those already caregiving, and offer insight to the many who don't know today that this may be their life, and their story, tomorrow."
~ **Rosalynn Carter**, former First Lady and President of the Board of Directors of the Rosalynn Carter Institute for Caregiving at Georgia Southwestern State University, Americus, GA

"*Jan's Story* will offer solace and support to others as they seek support systems while enduring the 24/7 agony of watching a life partner transformed into some "other," who then gradually vanishes completely before one's very eyes."
~ **Sam Gandy, M.D., Ph.D.**, Chairman Emeritus, National Medical and Scientific Advisory Council, Alzheimer's Association, Mount Sinai Chair in Alzheimer's Disease Research, Professor of Neurology and Psychiatry Mount Sinai School of Medicine

"This is one of the most honest portrayals of caring for someone with Alzheimer's disease I've read. This is not just a book about loss, it is a book about hope."
~ **Darby Morhardt, MSW, LCSW.** Research Associate Professor and Director – Education, Cognitive Neurology and Alzheimer's Disease Center, Northwestern University Feinberg School of Medicine

"Read it for solace, read it for knowledge, but mostly read it so you know millions are also treading this difficult journey, too."
~ **Kathleen Kelly**, Executive Director of the National Center on Caregiving, a program of the Family Caregiver Alliance, San Francisco, CA

"An intimate look into a man's life, caring for his beloved wife, and surviving the heart-wrenching ordeal imposed by The Disease."
~ **Mark Warner**, Gerontologist, *The Alzheimer's Daily News*, author of *The Complete Guide to Alzheimer's-Proofing Your Home* and *In Search of the Alzheimer's Wanderer*

"*Jan's Story* is a love story trapped in a travesty, but one from which we can all learn to heal our hearts."
~ **Newt Gingrich**, Co-Chair of Alzheimer's Study Group and Founder of The Center for Health Transformation, former Speaker of the U.S. House of Representatives

"It is impossible to read this book without wanting to help fight this disease. As a laboratory scientist…it is easy to avoid confronting the personal loss experienced by the patient and family. There is no avoiding the personal effects of disease in *Jan's Story*."
~ **George A. Carlson, Ph.D.**, Director and Researcher, McLaughlin Research Institute, Great Falls, MT

"Barry's beautifully told love story of two healthy, vibrant, adventurous people is made more heartbreaking by the desolation caused when family and friends misjudged that Jan had been abandoned. Barry's story will help people understand how the brain can die very slowly while the body still looks healthy and, on some days, can appear normal."
~ **Elaine Jones,** COO, Allen Institute for Brain Science

Jan's Story

Love Lost to the Long Goodbye of Alzheimer's

by
Barry R. Petersen

Behler
PUBLICATIONS
California
USA

Behler Publications
California

Jan's Story
A Behler Publications Book

Copyright © 2010 by Barry R. Petersen
Cover design by Cathy Scott – www.mbcdesigns.com
Front cover photo used with permission by Erick H. Petersen

"Chronic Stress Can Steal Years From Caregivers' Lifetimes" (c) Prof. Jan Kiecolt-Glaser, quoted with permission of the author

Author photo used with permission from John Carman

Library of Congress Cataloging-in-Publication Data

Petersen, Barry (Barry Rex), 1949-
  Jan's story : love lost to the long goodbye of Alzheimer's / by Barry Petersen and Jan Chorlton Petersen.
    p. cm.
  ISBN-13: 978-1-933016-44-3 (softcover)
  ISBN-10: 1-933016-44-2 (softcover)
  1. Petersen, Jan Chorlton, 1949---Mental health. 2. Alzheimer's disease--Patients--Colorado--Biography. 3. Journalists--United States--Biography. 4. Petersen, Jan Chorlton, 1949- I. Title.
  RC523.2.P48 2010
  362.196'8310092--dc22
  [B]

                        2010001261

SECOND PRINTING

ISBN 13: 1-933016-44-3
e-book ISBN 978-1-933016-97-9

Published by Behler Publications, LLC
Lake Forest, California
www.behlerpublications.com

Manufactured in the United States of America

To everyone who reached out with a phone call, an e-mail, a letter, a hug.

And to the one who ever so gently pulled me back from the abyss, and then patiently taught me what every caregiver who cries through night's darkness needs to know.

You are not alone.

"I call heaven and earth to witness against you today, that I have set before you life and death, the blessing and the curse. So choose life in order that you may live, you and your descendants."

Deuteronomy 30:19
New American Standard Bible

Foreword by Katie Couric

My colleague, Barry Petersen, and I share something that we both work hard at, and take much pride in, and that is being television news journalists. We also share something in our personal lives that is difficult for both of us; losing our spouses. Jay was just 42 when he died of colon cancer in 1998. One of the many ways I have honored his life is working to encourage every American 55 and over to have a colonoscopy.

Barry is enduring a similar loss, but in a very different way. His lovely wife, Jan, has Early Onset Alzheimer's Disease, and Barry wrote *Jan's Story* to show the terrible impact this disease imposes not just on the person with the diagnosis, but also on the caregiver and the family.

The growing toll of Alzheimer's Disease was brought in to sharp focus for Americans when former President Ronald Reagan shared with all of us that he had the disease. On November 5, 1994, he released a handwritten letter. This is part of what he said:

I have recently been told that I am one of the Americans who will be afflicted with Alzheimer's Disease. In the past Nancy suffered from breast cancer and I had my cancer surgeries. We found through our open disclosures, we were able to raise public awareness. We were happy that as a result many more people underwent testing. They were treated in early stages and able to return to normal, healthy lives.

So now, we feel it is important to share it (Alzheimer's Disease) with you. In opening our hearts, we hope this might promote greater awareness of this condition. Perhaps it will encourage a clearer understanding of the individuals and families who are affected by it.

It was brave for President Reagan to be this open. He and Nancy knew that people would forever see him in a different light after his admission. But he also believed that his decision could show us all something about honesty in facing the disease that was devastating his mind and robbing him of his memories. The way he shared his personal story with the world encouraged others to be open with their family and friends and not treat Alzheimer's as some kind of shameful secret.

President Reagan's disease came late in life. Early Onset Alzheimer's Disease is about youth and dreams cut short. *Jan's Story* will give you a clearer understanding of what happens when Alzheimer's attacks someone so young. Jan was only 55 when she was formally diagnosed, although she showed symptoms for years.

As their journey unfolds, there is another story here, and this one is about Barry. Like others dealing with this disease at such an early age, he struggled to care for his beautiful wife and to also find ways that he could go on living.

It is a challenge for those left behind; a combination of guilt because you are the survivor, and the natural instinct to move forward. We do not want to forget the ones we loved so deeply, but we also want to find a balance between the past and the urgent need to go on with life for ourselves and the loved ones in our lives who depend on us.

This book can help those who have come to this terrible crossing because they can now appreciate the fact that they are not alone. And those who have not personally experienced this disease will find a story that will help them understand what others have endured.

Jan's Story is about understanding the difficulty and pain of being left behind. We live and love believing that we have many years ahead of us. When the person we have loved leaves us, we need to find strength and go on, day by day.

As Barry writes, all of us learn, in time, to accept that our beloveds would wish us to have a second chance at life, just as we would wish that for them. We do that while never forgetting what we once had and cherished . . . what we once had and lost.

Katie Couric is anchor and managing editor of the **CBS Evening News with Katie Couric** *and correspondent for* **60 Minutes**

The Disease

"In Alzheimer's Disease, as in other types of dementia, increasing numbers of nerve cells deteriorate and die. A healthy adult brain has 100 billion nerve cells, or neurons, with long branching extensions connected at 100 trillion points . . . called synapses . . .

"Different strengths and patterns of signals move constantly through the brain's circuits, creating the cellular basis of memories, thoughts and skills.

"In Alzheimer's Disease, information transfer at the synapses begins to fail, the number of synapses declines and eventually cells die.

"Brains with Alzheimer's Disease show dramatic shrinkage from cell loss and widespread debris from dead and dying neurons."

Alzheimer's Association
2009 Alzheimer's Disease Facts and Figures
"More about Alzheimer's Disease"
Page Seven

Percentage Changes in
Selected Causes of Death 2000 and 2006

Heart Disease	Percentage change	- 11.5
Breast Cancer	Percentage change	- 2.6
Prostate Cancer	Percentage change	- 8.7
Stroke	Percentage change	- 18.2
Alzheimer's Disease	Percentage change	+ 46.1

SOURCE: Alzheimer's Association, 2010 - Alzheimer's Disease Facts and Figures

~From Barry~

I never intended to write this book. I saved my notes and my "Jan Updates" and the e-mails people sent me so I could read and remember how Jan was on this day or that.

It was also my way of measuring how I was losing her. And with these notes, I could forever go back and keep alive, in my memory, the shared moments she has lost.

You will find in this book a wonderful, loving and accomplished woman . . . My Jan.

I hope you will understand why my journey could not end with Alzheimer's taking her away. And if you understand that, you will know why I came to write this. For those caught in this never-ending twilight, perhaps there will be guidance here, if only in knowing you are not alone.

I now entrust this chronicle to you. You will read the choices I made driven by every human's strongest needs . . . love and survival.

Some will take heart, some will condemn. This is up to you.

I offer only this: I believe that by sharing this journey, and by living beyond Jan's battle with Early Onset Alzheimer's Disease, I honor her.

My Jan.

Prologue

"Every man's memory is his private literature."
~*Aldous Huxley*

May I tell you the story of how I never proposed to Jan? No getting down on bended knee, no diamond ring in a box—because I was so broke after a divorce that I couldn't afford a ring.

No Jan sitting in some fancy restaurant, choking up, blurting out a joyful "Yes." We had been friends for a while because she worked at the CBS TV affiliate in Seattle and I would travel there for stories, often working out of their newsroom.

One evening . . . the first time she ever invited me to her tiny one-bedroom apartment overlooking Lake Washington . . . we sat and talked. It was never more than that . . . sorry . . . no scenes that censors would take out of the movie version.

It was just that, somehow, we knew - both of us - that we would be together from then on, HAD to be together.

I gently kissed her goodnight and walked away and felt as if I had been in an earthquake. I was shaken and elated, scared, but also ecstatic with the sense of being alive . . . I knew my life had changed in brilliant ways.

We were married in San Francisco on Valentine's Day in 1985, and then lived here and there across the globe . . . San Francisco, Tokyo, Moscow, London and back to Tokyo and Beijing.

My job as a journalist for CBS News provided Jan and me with the ability to see and experience the world. Much of it was wonderful, some of it still gives me nightmares.

In Sarajevo one day, a mortar round hit near where the crew and I were standing outside by our armored car. Two people were killed and a piece of shrapnel buried itself in our armored car inches away from where I was standing. We went there to do a job . . . we reported on the old women and children killed and we dodged the same sniper fire.

In the aftermath of the Rwanda genocide, I was sent to cover the thousands who fled to a volcanic plain in what is now the Democratic Republic of Congo. Soon thereafter, a cholera epidemic broke out and people died for lack of a gallon of water and some salt. How many bodies do you see stacked up near mass graves that are being dug by bulldozers before you lose count and forget? I did a story at an orphanage where we knew the littlest and sickest babies would be dead in a few hours before the story even aired back in the US.

I did it and I coped.

But the week when I had to fly from Tokyo to Seattle by myself and arrange for Jan to move into an assisted living facility, a place I was told she should probably never leave . . . that was when I learned how a man can fall to the floor because he is weeping so hard.

I had already lost so much of her. But this was arranging for her move to America while I remained in Asia. This was the physical reality of what Alzheimer's had taken from her mind and from me.

Here is part of the note I sent out that weekend to friends explaining my decision. It captures the part I hated most. I was her husband, her lover and her best friend, and I felt that I was failing her.

I am now being dragged down in ways which will start affecting my health and well being, if it hasn't already. This is not unusual for caregivers, and studies show that being an Alzheimer's caregiver to a loved one can shorten your life rather dramatically.

I am just barely smart enough that -- when it is pointed out -- I can and do see what is happening to me, such as my deepening level of exhaustion or the effects of living on a never-ending emotional roller coaster. I am reliably informed that if I do not make this change, and soon, this will not end well for me. And while my welfare is secondary because, in this battle, we must all put Jan first, there is logic to knowing that if I falter and fail, she will suffer for it.

I once told friends that I would trade my soul for Jan to be healed, and they shushed me . . . worried that the devil's demon Mephistopheles who bested Dr. Faustus might hear.

If he is listening, the offer still stands.

Walking Into Oblivion: Stage One

No impairment (normal function)
Unimpaired individuals experience no memory
problems and none are evident to a health care
professional during a medical interview. (Seven Stages
of Alzheimer's Disease from www.alz.org, the
Alzheimer's Association)

It seemed strange that the first Stage of Alzheimer's is about showing no obvious symptoms. The answer lies within the disease, an answer that offers the additional terror that Alzheimer's is already at work before a person knows it or before an expert like a doctor can tell.

This is how it was with Jan. Then as time went on and I thought back about our life together, the clues were there, but only in hindsight. Alzheimer's has immense patience as it creeps. It oozes with such stealth that some researchers now believe it starts twenty or thirty years before the symptoms are obvious enough for diagnosis. It begins in the cradle of everything that is us, in a healthy brain.

Jan was perfectly healthy. We had physicals every year, and she always did better than I. She was from a family that considered living past ninety as normal. She exercised her brain as a marvelous writer, far better than I. She read voraciously, everything from the morning paper to magazines on design, art, travel, and antiques. She was always well dressed with her hair beautifully styled. She traveled easily and occasionally repeated herself. It was easy not to see if you started out not wanting to see.

Jan was always younger looking than her years, always upbeat. She could chat with anyone and they would feel better for it. She had a strong and optimistic personality.

One can hide a lot behind optimism.

1

To the Looking-Glass world it was Alice that said
"I've a scepter in hand, I've a crown on my head.
Let the Looking-Glass creatures, whatever they be
Come dine with the Red Queen, the White Queen and Me!"
~Lewis Carroll/From Chapter IX of "Through the Looking Glass"

First Days

It happened on a balmy Tokyo summer weekend of 2005. I had to leave our Tokyo apartment after breakfast on a Saturday morning for a story on robots. Jan was up with me, making us omelets and coffee as we chatted over the morning papers.

When I came home that afternoon, Jan had walked through the Looking Glass, disappearing into the world of Early Onset Alzheimer's Disease. She stayed there for three days.

Mostly I remember her eyes, unusually wide open and intense, staring hard, and directly at me, and yet seemingly without comprehension. At one point I thought she was having a stroke so I had her raise and lower her arms. She seemed physically fine.

During those three days she heard voices in our apartment telling her that people were coming to dinner and other voices at the grocery store telling her what to buy. She made sentences with all the correct words, but they were out of order. (Try it sometime - it is remarkably difficult.)

She couldn't remember people's names so she described them by their appearance, such as "that skinny man you work with."

Despite my trying to dissuade her that no company was coming, she made dinner for three people one night, carefully putting food on three plates.

At bedtime, she dressed in layers of street clothes, not her normal silk pajamas.

When a spam advertising message popped up on the computer as an "alert," she found pen and paper and wrote it down word for word, then told me it was a warning of danger. The third night, she went to make hamburgers. She put the hamburgers into a deep pot normally used to boil water for pasta, then used a frying pan as a lid, turned the burner to maximum heat and walked into the bedroom saying she was tired and was going to take a nap. I jumped up and turned off the stove.

Because we lived in Tokyo at the time, we were in a different time zone than the United States. It was 4 a.m. in Tokyo when I finally reached a neurologist in San Francisco and described the symptoms.

"From what you say, she has Early Onset Alzheimer's Disease," the doctor said. "There will be good days and bad days."

I objected. How could the doctor be so sure, and over the phone at that?

"She has Alzheimer's Disease," the doctor said with flat-voiced finality.

On the morning of day four, Jan was fine, seemingly back to normal, with no memory of what had happened. To her, those days simply didn't exist in her mind. Maybe it was better this way. Some people slide slowly into this disease, faltering at work or at home, leaving friends and loved ones to raise eyebrows or ask questions.

For some unknown reason, and as I learned more about this disease, I heard the word "unknown" a lot. I had three days of seeing into the future; what Jan would be like someday in the months or years ahead, and no one could tell me how soon or how long. That is the hardest unknown.

The next steps were familiar ones . . . the visit to the San Francisco neurologist and the tests that couldn't tell us anything with certainty. They strapped electrodes to her head and took readings. Everything came back normal, which meant nothing.

Somewhere, early on, a doctor told me: "We can't really know for sure if it is Alzheimer's until she is dead and we do an autopsy on the brain."

Dead? When did dead come in?

Now I felt panic. How soon could this kill her? Another unknown.

How fast is the progression? Depends.

What medications will work? No way of predicting, no idea how effective. They don't cure, they don't even stop it. They are like a man on the railroad track trying to hold back a slow moving locomotive with all his strength . . . but the train edges forward, always forward.

The Disease progresses no matter how hard you push back.

If I had to paint a picture of my life in those first weeks and months, it would look like something from kindergarten. I would take all the beautiful colors of Jan; our experiences and remembrances, our plans and dreams, our intense love, the sound of her voice, how she felt in my arms, how in the middle of the night when she was asleep I could snuggle against her back and she would readjust to fold tight against me and then I could wrap my arms around her.

And I would twist the brush in vicious strokes, back and forth, until all those beautiful colors were a mix of bright and dark that no longer makes sense.

Together we built a life, made friends, hunted for treasures in antique stores, traveled and loved the new experiences. Our lives made sense. And then, with the coming of The Disease, all of that was taken away and in its place was unpredictability, and loss.

I was not alone. One doctor told me that Early Onset Alzheimer's can strike people as young as thirty.

And, as the incidence of over-all Alzheimer's explodes in the United States, so will the number of Early Onset cases. At the moment, about 5.3 million Americans have Alzheimer's. Of those, an estimated 10%, or half a million, suffer Early Onset or other forms of dementia, which means those diagnosed with Alzheimer's who are under sixty-five.

And projections from the Alzheimer's Association are that by 2050 the number of those with Alzheimer's Disease could triple to 16 million.

But of the millions, there was only one person I cared about at this moment . . . Jan

Can I describe her for you? I am not sure I can get it all.

Only five foot two, I nicknamed her The Shortblonde. I would swear she was born with a smile, and never stopped laughing. By the time I met her she was one of the prime news anchors at KIRO-TV, a Seattle TV station. True to her spunky nature, she always had a bountiful supply of grit and exuberance, and that helped her success. But she made it the hard way by starting as a part time writer and working her way up. Before too long, she moved up to being a producer, then a reporter, and finally an anchorwoman.

She brought a spirit of optimism to our lives, one that helped her accept her role as wife and the added job of stepmother. It was a challenge and yet, she made it tolerable for me and fun for my two daughters.

When she first met them they were two and seven. To her, when the girls were with us, we were the Dad and Jan family. She made it seem that way naturally. She plotted wonderful vacations for us all—once putting us on a one-year savings plan to pay for an African safari.

She helped me survive the girls' teenage years because she had been a teenage girl. They could be moody around me, and I would be sympathetic. Jan would know better, and tell them they were perfectly capable of creating their own good moods. And as for helping two teenagers with critical knowledge . . . clothes, makeup, boys . . . she handled easily what I could not have handled at all.

And, always, she made it seem easy to them. The occasional anger and frustration that comes with raising kids was something she shared with me, and I with her, and not with the girls. It would have made them feel bad, and making people feel terrible was not something she would do.

She dressed beautifully and tried hard to make me do the same. She loved picking out my clothes, especially suits and shirts and lovely ties. It never bothered her that I hated spending money on myself. She spent it on me with a mischievous smile, and a nearby clerk would happily process the credit card.

No matter where we lived, and we moved every few years, she draped our apartments with fabrics of warm colors and surrounded us with the antiques we found together, or silly mementos of trips taken and places lived.

To her, life was bright and good. Her favorite colors—rich, full reds and golds and soft warm pinks.

Jan was fifty-five-years old when she was diagnosed that night at 4 a.m. Tokyo time. We had been married for twenty years.

The doctors call it Early Onset Alzheimer's Disease. Perhaps it is good to have a name for a disease that will rob and cheat and steal and slowly suck the person you love away from you.

There is a line from the movie *An Affair to Remember* that goes: "Winter must be cold for those with no warm memories."

Soon, for Jan, there will no longer be the memories of us, the warmth of our love.

Soon, for Jan, every day will be a cold and lonely winter.

TIMELINE
September, 2005
Jan's e-mail to a friend about her diagnosis

Ellen! Andre!

Everything fine here, with the surprise exception I never expected; turns out that recently, after a few days of my being somewhat "wacky" we took me off for a check up and here's the good/bad news . . . I've been diagnosed with (Early Onset) Alzheimer's. Don't know how or why . . . doesn't run in my family, etc., so I can't figure this out . . . however, the really GOOD news is that we live in the age of miracles . . . instead of being doomed to being shut in the attic, I am blessed with a bushel basket of pills which I now RELIGIOUSLY take . . . morning and evening . . . and as far as I can tell (well, actually it's BARRY who is my weather vane) it appears that the triumph of medicine is WORKING!

I know it SOUNDS GHASTLY . . . but as Barry will tell you, I am now my usual self thanks to the miracle of meds . . . and long may they reign!

So in the "Don't Cry for Me Argentina" mode . . . this does entail my carrying around the assorted pills, but hey! Consider the alternatives! I'm all for pills . . . morning and evening . . . the neurologist is pretty clear on what I can and can't do, which principally means I will never, ever miss a pill . . . but that's not such a big deal . . . and as it turns out there are all kinds of researchers out there trying to develop even BETTER meds for all of us "boomers" . . . talk about the world's largest captive audience!

Love, Jan

2

"The leaves of memory seemed to make
A mournful rustling in the dark."
~Henry Wadsworth Longfellow

About Jan

Every couple's life is their own private novel. It is a little personal history added day by day, experiences that can be remembered later with a word or even a look. Someone else talks about visiting some place . . . and with a glance at each other you can remember being there, the two of you.

Our private novel was about happiness and love. As simple as that.

She had favorite stories.

"Do you know when my dad was born?" she would ask friends who clearly did not. "He was born on January 14th. And one of my brothers was born on January 14th. And you know who else? Barry was born on January 14th!"

It was Capricorn destiny, proof that we were fated to be.

Her favorite story was how we first met, in the newsroom at the Seattle TV station where she was working as a reporter and anchor. I was there covering a US Senate race for the CBS Evening News. This was before the days of laptop computers. I had commandeered her desk and typewriter and was frantically working on a script against a tight deadline. Jan came back into the newsroom from an assignment.

"I walked in and saw this *man* sitting at my desk," Jan would say. "I walked up and told him, 'this is my desk, and I need it because I have to write my story.'"

Then came the part she loved the most. "He looked up at me, and he RIPPED his paper out of the typewriter and stomped away."

When she can remember, it always makes her laugh. I didn't laugh at the time it happened and not for a while afterwards. But in time it became one of my favorite stories about us. It reminded me of how she was pretty and spunky and totally unimpressed by me, the big-time network news correspondent who was a touch too impressed with himself.

I blessed the day we were married and look at the wedding picture of our blended futures . . . Jan and me and my two daughters, Emily (7) and Julie (2), from my first marriage. When I look at the pictures from that night, I see in her face a radiated joy, a kind of total, sheer happiness that I never believed I could give a woman, and yet it seemed natural. My smile is real and, if you look closely, maybe a bit unbelieving that someone this amazing was about to become my wife. Until her, I had never believed a man could be that happy, and I definitely never thought it would be me. But she made it so.

It was going to be a struggle combining the girls, Jan, and me into one family, but we thought it was exciting. We both knew it would be complicated, and we both had no doubts that in the end it would be fine.

Because we had each other. That is what *fine* is all about.

There were plenty of real life concerns in our early days. It was 1985, and my bank account was pretty much empty from my divorce and the legal fees. At the time, I was based in the CBS News Bureau in San Francisco. Our love triggered her life-changing moment.

She was in Seattle and quit her job. We needed to be together. I drove up in my second-hand Oldsmobile, rented a U-Haul trailer, and we packed her small apartment and moved her to where I was, and to where we would make our lives one.

We managed to scrape some money together and buy a tiny house in San Francisco in a neighborhood called Eureka Valley which was, as quirky San Francisco goes, not in a valley at all, but on a hill. And not just a hill, but a steep, steep hill up from the Castro District of San Francisco.

Our house was one of several ticky-tacky row houses built in the 1950s for policemen or teachers as affordable housing in the city. We loved it because it was a part of the city, perfectly plain and a touch ugly on the outside since it was devoid of any architectural charm. It was a box with windows in a series of houses that looked like boxes all running together. The outside paint job stayed with the theme of very ordinary . . . beige. I remember thinking that even the roof was boring . . . perfectly flat.

I loved it because I could almost afford it, and Jan loved it because it was ours. The main floor was a living and dining room and a true 1950s kitchen. And the best part was that it came with a small corner fireplace in the living room. Upstairs had the only bathroom and three amazingly compact bedrooms. Each floor, divided up as it was into different rooms, had just slightly more total space than our two-car garage on the street level.

It had been a rental house when we bought it, so it was wanting for love and care. Every wall needed paint. But we didn't mind since all the work was just another part of making it ours.

From the first floor at night, as the fog slipped over the western hills and started toward the city, we could look out our living room windows and watch the first strands   drifting down our street. Then came the real gusts and finally, we would all but lose the houses across the street.

Upstairs, the largest bedroom faced the street and seemed the perfect master bedroom. From the windows, we could see over the neighbors' roofs and on to downtown; City Hall, the Bay Bridge, the San Francisco Bay itself. I thought how wonderful to put our bed in this room and wake up each morning to the glittering city of San Francisco.

And so we did. We lasted maybe two nights.

The steep hill we lived on started several blocks down from us, so by the time a car reached the street in front of our house, it was deep down into first gear and struggling against an almost 45-degree incline, transmission grinding and engine at full throttle. All night long, we would be tossed awake by yet another mechanical assault on the top of the hill.

We finally retreated to the back bedroom, a space so small that we could just fit our queen sized bed with one side flush against the wall. That meant we had to climb onto the bed to get the covers straightened on that side. But it was quiet.

Good things happened in that bedroom. And in the morning the sun would pour in.

Downstairs, carefully detailed wooden molding ran along the ceiling in the living/dining area, cupids, flowers or such—a touch of art in an otherwise cardboard box of a house.

"I'm going to paint it," Jan announced one day. "Pink and gold."

Along the way, she added blue to the mix, working slowly and carefully, highlighting the different parts of the molding. For weeks, she climbed a ladder each day with tiny brushes and painted. She added elegance to the space.

"It's all about colors," she explained to me, the person who did not study art history in college.

And "all about color" was why she painted the walls her favorite color . . . a pale pink.

"They use this color in mental institutions," she explained one day, which caught me by surprise. "It helps calm people. Don't you feel calmer?"

Well, of course.

Nothing escaped our attention, not even the hardwood floors, which we had refinished and polished to a bright sheen.

So when our day was over and the fog poured down our street, we would sit on the sofa in our (calm) little house and light a fire. We dimmed the lights and opened a bottle of champagne because life was good, and another day together was more than enough reason for a celebration.

Jan got part time work at the local NBC-TV affiliate, as a reporter and occasional anchor. One day she did a story on an urban Boy Scout troop having a summer campout on the rooftop of a San Francisco skyscraper, and the next day I found myself doing exactly the same story for the CBS Evening News.

That was a good night by the fireplace.

We were the Darling-Darling couple, because that's what we called each other. At Christmas, our presents to each other would be "From Darling, To Darling."

When I called and she heard my voice, it was always: "Darling!" She was always happy to hear from me, whether I was calling from somewhere else in the world where I was on assignment, or from the office to chat about dinner.

Her parents (mine were long since gone) teased us because we always kissed. "That will end when the honeymoon wears off," they said confidently.

But it didn't.

I am the child of a rocky marriage and a mother who struggled with the twin demons of alcoholism and chronic depression so serious she needed electro-shock therapy. Her struggles made for a difficult childhood and made me shy, reticent, and often suspicious of the world. Not Jan. If we passed someone begging on the street, and she felt the person was truly in need, she gave money. If she had none, she would give me that look and I dug into my pockets and put money into the cup or glass or hat.

Jan developed her taste for exploring the world early because her father was a globe-trotting vice president for Boeing, selling jetliners in China and Singapore and across Asia. It seemed normal to her that Dad would be gone for weeks and come home from places that, once she learned about them, were worthy of her curiosity and fueled her desire to visit.

She was the oldest of five and grew up taking care of brothers and sisters. They all grew up in the same house that was forever being remodeled as they got bigger and their needs changed. Summers as a kid meant out the door in the morning to the pool or to play with friends and then race back for meals. College was the University of Washington across town.

While in college, she scrimped and saved so she could travel around Europe one summer with friends. She loved it. They had no itinerary — when they got tired of one place they would take a train to somewhere else. It was the kind of trip that only those open to adventure could experience.

Adventure and travel may have been part of my appeal to her. Our life together was always about me coming and going on stories, or us coming and going on trips.

We came together because of our sureness about being a couple. There was no anticipation of adventure outside of the good things that happened when we were together.

But adventure came calling and we couldn't wait to see what was coming next. But adventure is like a coin – it can have two sides, one good, one devastating. For us, it would be both.

Walking Into Oblivion: Stage Two

Individuals may feel as if they have memory lapses, especially in forgetting familiar words or names or the location of keys, eyeglasses or other everyday objects. But these problems are not evident during a medical examination or apparent to friends, family or co-workers. (Seven Stages of Alzheimer's Disease from www.alz.org, the Alzheimer's Association)

Most people think of Alzheimer's as a disease of the old. They have a story of a relative . . . a grandparent, a great aunt, a distant and aged uncle . . . whose elderly life in their seventies or nineties ended in the solitary desolation of this disease. But youth is no protection. The Disease can strike people in their twenties or thirties. And when it strikes early, it can be unusually ravenous, quick and vicious.

And researchers say that Early Onset seems to move faster toward death. "It's as if they have the more malignant form of Alzheimer's disease," says Dr. Jeffrey Cummings, director of the UCLA Alzheimer's Disease Center. "It comes on earlier, and it lasts a shorter period of time, and leads to death sooner."

As an example of ravenous, quick, and vicious, consider the story of Mark Priddy, the subject of an article in a London newspaper in July, 2009.

Mark was an ordinary guy, remembered for being "super fit." When his symptoms began, he was initially diagnosed with depression. When he was thirty-three, doctors determined that he had Early Onset Alzheimer's Disease. Mark and Dione (his wife) had two daughters. By the age of forty, he could no longer speak, walk, or feed himself.

When I think of the clues strewn across our past that Jan had Alzheimer's, one of them was her fading ambition. She had always worked, from college onward and during most of the early years of our marriage. When we lived together in San

Francisco from 1984 to 1986, she worked for the local NBC affiliate as reporter and fill-in anchor. It was the same when we moved overseas...and then it wasn't.

I never dreamed this had anything to do with Alzheimer's Disease. There was no reason early on to make that leap, and every reason as time went by to deny it.

And as time went by, denial was a much crafted, much practiced art for us both.

3

*"In Russia we only had two TV channels. Channel One was
propaganda. Channel Two consisted of a KGB officer telling
you: Turn back at once to Channel One."*
~Yakov Smirnoff

If Someone Said Adventure, Count Jan In

In the spring of 1986, a year into our marriage, CBS News
offered me the job as their Tokyo correspondent. The original
assignment was supposed to last two years, but somehow we
just kept going around the globe – from Tokyo to Moscow, then
to London and back to Tokyo for a second posting.

It meant giving up our San Francisco house and lifestyle,
and the comfort of living in a country where we could speak the
language and understand the culture. But Jan embraced it as if
this was exactly what she signed up for, and when do we begin.

She had no doubts that we would be fine, would settle in
and could figure out the rest as it came along. I said yes, based
on her confidence and her sheer excitement for the unknown. I
couldn't turn it down once Jan got excited. If she could make it
work for both of us – and she was sure she could – the least I
could do was agree and call the movers.

Jan loved Tokyo and its sense of the exotic East, but the next
call to move on was not so good because Moscow was the capital
of a culture she came to hate, despite that spirit of adventure.
"The Russians feel sorry for themselves all the time." It was said
as much in sadness as simple observation. She believed strongly
about creating good in your own life. I tried to gently remind her
that we had a few more advantages than the average Russian.

"I don't know," she insisted. "I think they just love being
depressed." She could never seem to comprehend why someone
would choose "being depressed." To her, life was about finding
the good in each day and each experience, no matter how trying.

But in Russia, people seemed on a centuries-long course of endless tragedy. It made for great, if agonizing, literature and extraordinary classical music. But the sense of gloom rubbed up against Jan's very nature. She believed that each person made their own happiness, and she believed that especially for the two of us. If we had chances to see or do new things, it was up to us to seize those moments and make them ours.

We had a kitchen large enough for an old wooden table and chairs suitable for breakfast and, on cold Russian winter nights, we would sit with a bowl of borscht and be happy for the warmth of the stove and the cooking. The rest of the rooms were big and simple . . . one for dining, another as a living room, and one large single bedroom. German prisoners of war had been used to construct the building, and it was solid, with some interior walls almost three feet thick.

Moscow was perfect for Jan's dinner-party organizing because most of us socialized in our homes. At that time the Soviet-era propagandists still touted Moscow as the glorious culmination of Communism. In fact, it was so *in*glorious that it had almost no functioning restaurants. By functioning, I mean the absolute bare minimum . . . clean and with safe, edible food. Instead, the food was badly, and sometimes barely, cooked. The cheese was dried and fly-stained because it had been left sitting out for hours, and the norm was service with a snarl. It was so bad that a business lunch would usually be a rendezvous at the American Embassy snack bar for a hamburger and a soda.

Case in point of how bad it was; one of the few hotels that catered only to foreigners had the city's only sushi restaurant, which was run by a Japanese company. But to be sure that the sushi was safe, we checked the schedule of the two Tokyo-to-Moscow flights each week and went to the restaurant the next day when the fish from Japan was fresh off the plane.

Another prime example of Moscow's culinary delights was the butcher's market around the corner from our apartment. Shoppers had to swat away the clouds of flies to get at the meat. Street vendors sold ice cream only in the worst of winter because they had no refrigeration, and the bitter cold was all that kept the ice cream frozen. Even so, we would not

buy ice cream from them or any other dairy products from the
grimy, dusty local stores that smelled of sour milk.

So we, as journalists, diplomats, and foreign business people,
entertained in our apartments, where the food was safe despite
the fact that our conversations were monitored by the KGB.
Shopping was a trick, and Jan, true to her nature, mastered it
quickly. To guarantee safe food, we had all our groceries shipped
in from nearby Finland, using a store that, for years, had
specialized in providing food and other necessities (toilet paper,
new tires for the bureau cars, bath towels, diapers, ball point pens)
to Moscow's foreigners like us.

Once a week Jan would take out pen and paper, go through
their grocery catalog and prepare the food order, right down to
meat and milk. About all we could trust to buy in Moscow was
bread and sometimes cabbage for borscht when it was in season.

Armed with her list, Jan went up to the office for a session
with the telex machine, basically a typewriter. It worked like a
phone in that we could dial another telex anywhere in the world.
These were the days before faxes, and in Moscow there were days
when the phones could barely transmit a voice. The order was
telexed off early in the week.

On Thursday, dozens of company drivers would head for the
train station to pick up the boxes of imported groceries shipped in
from Helsinki for their foreign bosses. If we were having people
for dinner, the pre-planning was far more extensive. And if you
forgot to order something, there was no place to run out to get it.
It either came in from Finland on the once-a-week train shipment,
or you did without, or you went sheepishly to a neighbor and
borrowed what you forgot to order.

Inviting friends to our apartment fueled Jan's enthusiasm for
cooking. Everyone, from our next-door neighbors coming for
Saturday night dinner, to visiting dignitaries looking to connect
with American journalists (and find an edible meal) were
welcome at our table. Al Gore, then a Tennessee senator, was in
Moscow on a trip investigating environmental issues, and a friend
brought him around to our place for lunch. He confessed that he
liked spicy food, which was also a huge favorite of Jan's.

She sliced some fresh Russian bread and pulled out a jar of
what I considered to be insanely hot sauce, which was a kind of

searing jelly concoction from a southern Soviet area. I thought the jelly might be strong enough to eat through the glass and certainly though the lining of the stomach. She knew it was a hit when the hot peppers made sweat pop out on Gore's forehead. They both had seconds.

Jan could just as easily plan and cook a formal dinner for twelve and loved the challenge. The rest of us would marvel at the result and, at the end of the evening we'd raise our glasses in a happy and noisy toast to Jan, the Chef.

Jan also brought her artistic touch to the flat, which was furnished. We could only bring clothes and a few paintings from Tokyo, so she picked out the most vibrant paintings, the ones with bright reds. And when we bought art work in Moscow to decorate, it was the same . . . splashes of color . . . as if the brightness of the flat inside could somehow neutralize Moscow's endless gray.

Our flat was bugged by the KGB, of course, and we had no choice but to live there since it was the company apartment assigned by the Soviet authorities. CBS News reporters and their families had lived there for decades. Each summer, the girls would come and spend two months with us, and we would befuddle the eavesdroppers by moving our bed into the dining room so the girls could have the bedroom.

And, within a night or two, we would hear the scraping, like a huge rat slowly creeping and crawling in the ceiling. "The idiots," Jan would say, half-delighted with their lack of subtlety. They were, of course, moving the listening devices through the crawl space in the ceiling from the bedroom to the dining room where we had moved the bed in the summer so they could listen in on our pillow talk.

At the end of summer the girls left, and we moved back into the bedroom. "Here it comes," Jan would say, all but laughing. And sure enough, the first or second night, we heard the scraping noises as they dragged the listening device from the dining room back to the bedroom. I can hear it, still. And when we talk about it, and when she remembers, it still makes her giggle.

Life could be tricky in Moscow, especially dealing with the authorities. We quickly learned that there were a lot of rules, mostly ignored, since the bureaucrats did what they wanted. Or sometimes, it seemed, they made up new rules, just for the occasion, and usually so they could say . . . *nyet.*

So we were nervous as we packed to leave Moscow for the next assignment in London. It meant direct dealings with the authorities, but Jan turned it into a total triumph. One of those dealings centered on getting our Soviet-era art out of Moscow, and it was one of her proudest moments. Each piece, including the few antiques we bought there, needed a special stamp from the Ministry of Culture approving it for export to make sure we weren't absconding with any state treasures. That meant a personal inspection visit from Ministry officials before anything could be packed.

Jan researched it well and had gift bags ready for the two women inspectors who showed up. The important gift was American-made Marlboro cigarettes, practically a currency of its own in the desperate poverty that was Moscow in those days. This was the era where the Soviets had so little in their lives that people would get in line sometimes not even knowing what the line was for; only that something might be available in a shop. Foreign goods were rare and, in some cases, dangerous to have.

The ladies from the Ministry were not initially that friendly and had the grim heavy look that came from too many potatoes and loaves of bread, and too little meat, which was the typical Soviet diet washed down by the ever-present vodka. At first they were authoritative, bordering on rude, and in no mood to help us in any way. But Jan found something they, from such different upbringings and points of life, had in common . . . a shared passion for art. And these women, who were so unpleasant at first, soon warmed to Jan and her enthusiasm for beauty and its expression in paintings. We had some art books and Jan pulled several off the shelf, including my single favorite—a massive coffee table book of paintings by Edward Hopper. The women had never seen his works.

When I came home for dinner, I found all five-foot-two of Jan standing proud. She told me about the visit and said they had softened when she showed the women our art books, especially the collections of works by Hopper.

"Which," I said, looking at the empty space in the shelf, "isn't there."

"Nope. I gave it away."

Now, this moment could have ended badly. "You gave it to them? My Hopper book?"

She smiled at me, rather self-satisfied, because she knew this story was going to end well. "Look," she said, walking up to the first of our paintings. On the back, it had the stamp of approval for export. "See, here's another one." She laughed. "I got everything approved!"

I didn't laugh right away. After all, I loved that Hopper book. But she reminded me that we could buy Hopper books by the bushel outside of Moscow, and that these women had never seen his paintings. Their awe at his talent, their discovery of his work, trumped our having a book that we could easily replace. To Jan, it wasn't even a question, but an instinct, to share. Of course they had to have that book.

We laughed about that story later. I saw it as part of her ability to sense and understand people, which was invaluable to our nomadic way of life.

And it got all the art to London, where we ended up living in a tiny apartment near the CBS Bureau in Knightsbridge, down the street from Harrods and a quick cab ride to theaters and great shows.

It was a neighborhood, urban and exciting, with art galleries, restaurants and architecture from the many eras of London's lifetime. Everything we lacked in Moscow, we had in London . . . wonderful theater, a myriad of restaurants, pubs for unwinding on a Friday night and, as an extra bonus, we could speak the language.

We could walk five minutes to the Victoria and Albert Museum, or head off in a different direction to watch the Changing of the Guard at Buckingham Palace, or wander over to Hyde Park to feed the swans.

These were hard, dangerous days for any CBS News reporter based in the London Bureau. Our coverage area was all of Europe and Africa, and occasional duty in the Mideast including trips to Iraq. It meant spending a lot of time away from Jan — much of it in Sarajevo during the Bosnian War in the early 1990s, and in other places like Somalia.

Jan knew the stories and the risks and while she didn't like that last kiss before I headed off for an airplane, she knew I wanted to cover the stories, and she wanted that for me. She swallowed her fear, smiled and hugged, and let me go.

There were plenty of dangerous places, but when I was there the worst was probably Bosnia. Sarajevo snarled with sniper fire and shuddered from artillery shells that were lobbed into the city on a daily basis. The Holiday Inn was home to visiting foreign reporters, and its one major drawback was that it was near the front lines, which ran through part of the city. That meant all the windows were shot out. We stayed in rooms on the back side where the sniper bullets usually couldn't reach us, but the mortar shells hitting around the hotel had blasted out the windows on the back side as well. Our news team traveled in armored cars and did stories on those who hadn't survived the day.

Sometimes people would die in ones and twos, sometimes in groups as mortar rounds dropped in, aiming for places like the central market where people gathered to buy what food they could find. No one in the city knew where the next shell would hit, and that was what made Jan perpetually frightened each hour I was in Bosnia and away from her.

Mortar rounds are insidious because they make no sound coming down. Tank rounds make a noise, a kind of whistling, which you hear before they hit. It gives you time to fall flat. It's a false sense of security, but you hang on to it. Since they are silent, there is no warning, no noise. One minute life is normal, then a blast and a second of shock. The mind is slow to grasp such instant chaos. The next sounds are the screams of the injured, or the gasps of the dying. There is something horrible about the screams, a guilty horror because they aren't yours.

In Sarajevo one day, the producer, sound man, and I stood outside the TV station where we worked. Fifty yards away, a mortar round made a direct hit on a small plot of spring flowers. I couldn't help but wonder about the person who had planted the flowers. Had they been seeking some kind of normalcy that defied the murderous insanity around them? Screams emanated from an elderly lady with a shopping bag of hard-won food, and her cries of terror went up my spine as she lay sprawled on the ground. Nearby, a man who had been on a bicycle lay on the ground a few feet away. He did not scream.

But through it all in Sarajevo, there was a spirit of civilization that people would not surrender. They were caught in the daily crossfire of war where shells and bullets could hit anywhere at any time. Yet they acted with a defiance that left me amazed at their courage and their refusal to give up their dignity. Some dressed and went to work, even if it meant sitting in offices without jobs to do, or working in stores without goods to sell.

That was not true in another war zone, Mogadishu, Somalia. This was a city ravaged, where buildings were stripped and even the underground electrical wires were ripped out by the desperate who sold the metal for scrap.

Here there was no spirit of civilization. It was too hard just being alive at the end of the day. Much of the chaos came from crazy, dangerous renegades who ate a plant called "khat" all day long. By the time afternoon rolled around, its amphetamine-like euphoria affected the gunmen who, with a glassy-eyed look in their eyes, drove wildly in their "Mad Max" jeeps armed with huge .50-caliber machine guns. They shot at anything that moved and laughed as they did it. Everywhere we went, we drove in our own "Mad Max" jeeps and hired bodyguards, who chewed khat along with the rest. It didn't inspire confidence since these guys were supposedly on our side.

We went out one day to do a standup, which is the part of the story where the reporter talks directly into the camera. We decided we needed to do a retake, so the next day we told the bodyguards we were going back to the same place. They informed us that we most certainly were not and, with nervous voices, told us why. They heard that the faction controlling that area spotted us the day before and gunmen were about to take us out, but we suddenly left. Our bodyguards assured us that going back to the area would give them a second chance to kill us.

We opted for a different location.

Despite all this, Jan never once said don't go. "It's your job and I'm also a journalist and I understand, darling." But her eyes always showed an almost primal relief when I came back through the door, especially after being gone two or three weeks or more.

She always sent her imaginary friend, a kind of elfin sprite, to watch over me. "He's on my shoulder," she said with confidence. "But he's going with you, and he will watch over you." One time as I was leaving she laughed about her protective spirit and I asked why. "He knows you're both going to Sarajevo," she said giggling, "so he's wearing a uniform."

Married friends told me that as the years together go by they can lose that spark, the energy that once made them irresistible to each other. That never happened to us. Maybe it was because my job and the stories I covered out of London changed and intensified our relationship. When I returned from a trip, I always called from the airport to tell her I was on the way home, on the way to her.

Whether we were in our flat in London or our apartment in Tokyo, she would hear the elevator coming and was often standing, pacing, waiting with the apartment door open . . . afraid that maybe I wasn't really coming back, that somehow she had gotten it wrong. "Darling!" she would say. "Is it really you?"

We would hold on to each other . . . hungry, desperate, eager. The apartment door would close behind us and sometimes our front hallway was as far as we got before we were tearing at each other, driven by equal parts relief and passion.

When it was over . . . when we could both breathe again . . . I sometimes felt foolhardy. I realized what I had in this life, how much better I felt being close to her, how I wanted to live forever so we could be together, yes, forever. I was sure we had so many adventures ahead.

Yet by accepting the assignments, by traveling to some of these places, I put myself at grave risk. People were shooting and killing each other, and they didn't much care if I or anyone else got in the way. I went, in large part, because I felt I would be okay. Journalists have this odd belief that it won't happen to them. And I had this other belief that Jan and I would never end. That we had forever.

What could possibly go wrong with the lucky couple, Darling and Darling?

Walking Into Oblivion: Stage Three

Alzheimer's can be diagnosed in some, but not all, individuals with these symptoms.

Friends, family or co-workers begin to notice deficiencies. Problems with memory or concentration may be measurable in clinical testing or discernible during a detailed medical interview. Common difficulties include word- or name-finding problems noticeable to family or close associates . . . reading a passage and retaining little material . . . losing or misplacing a valuable object . . . decline in ability to plan or organize. (Seven Stages of Alzheimer's Disease from www.alz.org, the Alzheimer's Association)

The symptoms were piling up. And while Jan was changing, I was like a rock . . . steady and solid in my absolute refusal to hear or see what was going on in front of me. It wasn't as if I lacked for examples.

My daughter Emily tells the story of shopping at the grocery store in Tokyo with Jan. There was some sort of special promotion and Jan won a DVD. Later, when they got back to the house, Jan found the DVD in the shopping bag and said, "Where did this come from?"

"Dad," Emily told me later, "she couldn't remember what happened half an hour earlier."

People comfort me now by saying my self-imposed blindness to what was happening wouldn't have mattered in the progression of The Disease. It wasn't as if we delayed treatment for cancer, where delay can kill. They are right, although it brings me no comfort.

And there was the selfish part. I didn't want to face the end of the dream, the end of Darling and Darling, the end of everything around which we had created a life. Jan didn't want to accept that there might be some problem, either. Even the diagnosis didn't change her mood in any noticeable way. It was as if she couldn't, or wouldn't, grasp what it meant, or the horror

ahead of us. Quite the opposite, she seemed as much in denial as
I was.

Had I accepted or realized; had I been wise enough to see
what was ahead, I would have changed the very course of our
lives. That is what denial does . . . it robs us of the moments that
might have been.

Can I detail them? The South Seas cruise that we talked
about and could have taken after we diligently saved up enough
credit card points, but somehow never found the time. The train
trip on the Orient Express from Paris to Venice where we would
have dressed for dinner and pretended we were back in the
1920s. Or just spending more time at our northern California
home, watching the waves and waiting for another sunset.

Had there been some firm timeline or deadline, we would
have done these things. Who wouldn't?

But The Disease doesn't work like that. It gnaws at the brain
with a pace that differs with every person, and sometimes it
surrenders back some of what it has taken, with an evil,
unpredictable subtleness that fuels a false hope that time is not
running out.

So we went on with the daily routine and put off those
special moments because we told ourselves that there was
always next year. Believing in a next year is a kind of comfort. It
meant we had pushed the problems she was having down the
road a bit, maybe even beaten them back, because if we had
plans for next year, that must have meant that Jan would be here
next year.

Surely, I said to myself, there is clear reasoning in that.

When we moved to Tokyo for the first posting in 1986, she
became the radio stringer for CBS News. In Moscow from 1988
until 1990, she had her own contract for doing both radio and TV
stories. She was the go-to reporter, always ready to do the quick
radio piece on breaking news or the longer, more complex
stories for CBS News Weekend News and Sunday Morning.

Then there came a change in the Moscow Bureau. CBS sent
out another reporter during our last year there. It didn't really
affect Jan because there was more than enough work for all of
us. But she got angry at the idea of competition, and although
that was understandable, the anger never faded. She never

adjusted to the situation, and she reacted in a way very odd for someone who relished taking on a challenge . . . she withdrew. She stayed in our apartment, in the same building and a few floors below the office. I accepted her anger and her solitude uneasily. I tried talking her out of it, and in another moment out of character for her, she refused and stayed angry and isolated in the apartment.

Now I look back and wonder . . . was that the beginning of her own suspicions that something was wrong, the beginning of her avoiding new challenges, so no one would notice the things she would have trouble doing? Was the arrival of a new reporter not a cause, but an excuse, to hide what she felt were faltering writing and reporting skills?

From 1990 to diagnosis in 2005 . . . fifteen years—within the timeline.

After we moved to London, living there from 1991 to 1995, she did occasional part-time work for CNN. First it was stories for their business unit. The material was hard for her to master because the stories were complicated. She switched to doing some part-time fill-in anchor work and that was better. Much of what she read was written by others. And the news she presented was formulaic and predictable, the usual updates on various stock markets, the same information each day with only the numbers changing.

She was up early—4 a.m. because of the shift she covered—which gave her time to dress beautifully. It was comfortable and familiar for Jan to follow patterns that she knew well, like the dressing up, which she once did for her old job as an anchor in Seattle. Then the job faded away, and she didn't seem to care. In truth, she seemed relieved. She said it was nice not working those early morning hours. But was this another sign of her closing down?

And there was another clue—she spent more and more time at home. This was great for me. I would call from some faraway place on assignment, and she was there. If not, she was there half an hour later having just run to the grocery store.

There were virtually no lunches with friends, no trips to museums, no long walks in Hyde Park next to where we lived, no desire to find a new part time job. I didn't notice it because I was always pleased finding her home when I needed to talk.

I would ask what she was doing in the apartment and she would answer brightly, "I'm filing things for taxes," or "I'm catching up on reading all the magazines," or "I'm sorting through the mail."

Did Jan sense that she was changing? She may have. It may have frightened her or made her feel inadequate. She may have started compensating many years ago. I can offer opinion but not fact, because I didn't see it. Or, more accurately, I didn't want to see it. It was easier that way. And she never talked about it.

After we moved from London back to Tokyo in 1995 for our second go-round there, she worked as a radio stringer for Voice of America — doing only a story or two a week. Because we had a radio setup in the apartment, she could work from home and read her reports from our family room. She never went out to cover a story because she didn't need to — or was it because she was afraid to?

Then she got a one-year contract as the Tokyo reporter for ABC News, which meant every day to the office. But the job was difficult because of a dispute with another Asia reporter. I offered to help her resolve it. We could fly to New York, I said over and over, and meet with the ABC people and get it sorted out. But she wasn't interested. She gutted it out and did what work she could and earned her money. By the end of the year, she was visibly relieved that it was over. "Now my stomach doesn't hurt anymore," she said.

She was changing, literally in front of me — a vibrant, successful broadcast journalist whose confidence and drive to succeed were ebbing away like a quiet midnight tide.

4

"There's no use in weeping, though we are condemned to part:
There's such a thing as keeping, a remembrance in one's heart."
~Charlotte Bronte

About Barry

The mortar round exploded about a hundred yards behind me. It was late afternoon. I ducked instinctively. "Insurgents," said Army Capt. Steve Gventer, the officer who was with us. "They probably saw us and were trying for a lucky shot."

That day the luck was mine. It was summer 2004, with the American presence in Iraq under daily siege across the country. We were doing a standup where I was talking on camera, in Sadr City, Baghdad, the then-heartbeat of the anti-American resistance. Control of Sadr City bounced between the US forces during the day and the insurgents, who almost always took it back at night.

Being away on long assignments that could go a month or more was a reality of Jan's and my life together. But Baghdad was different, one of the hardest for her. I was focused on getting ready for the trip, on making sure I had a good bullet-proof vest and helmet. I also called people who had been there, looking for story ideas and tips on coming home alive. Jan was calm in all of this, until it was time to leave. At breakfast, my sunny and constantly optimistic wife was almost non-talkative. It was so out of character that I told someone later it was like the IRS apologizing for the inconvenience and sending all your taxes back. It just never happens.

I called her from the various airports through the day as I made my way to the Middle East, and that night from Jordan before the next day's flight into Baghdad. Somewhere in there she recovered her breezy disposition, if only to keep me cheered

up. Of course nothing would happen to me, she said. Her sheer
faith would keep that from happening.

I knew that every night I was in Baghdad she would
wonder what I was doing hour by hour. Was I safe in the hotel,
or out in the streets on a story? Could she bear to turn on the TV
and watch the nightly news on London TV and see what was
unfolding that day and . . . did the news include any American
journalists who were killed?

This was a time in Baghdad when journalists were targets
for kidnap, shot, or murdered. Some of our people spent their
entire time in Baghdad holed up inside the Al Monsour Hotel,
where the CBS News office was located. A big part of the budget
was our security.

There was outer security—Iraqi guards with AK47s at all
entrances including the parking lot—and inner security, the men
hired from a British firm who were trained by the British Army
in how to save their lives and, hopefully, ours. They were well
armed and less obvious about it.

The head of our British security team was nicknamed
Smudge. He had a chat with me the first day I arrived and
explained that he would be in the front seat of the heavily
armored Mercedes whenever we went out on a story. He also
taught me how we would handle trouble when we were outside
the car. "If one or two people are coming at us, I'll shoot them,"
he said in a tone I considered a bit matter-of-fact considering this
was my life under discussion. "If it's a big crowd, I'm not going
to open fire because they'll overwhelm us anyway, and it'll just
make them angrier. We surrender and see what can be done
next." Those were his rules of engagement, and they became
mine as well.

For seven weeks I worked the Iraq story, living on
cigarettes (I started smoking the second I hit that place) and
cookies. No alcohol. I wanted to be alert since we might need to
flee the hotel at any hour. Heavily armed men storming hotels at
3 a.m. where journalists or officials stayed was a new tactic then.

And once outside, the fear and no small amount of paranoia
crept in. I would see a couple of guys talking at the corner and
look up and stare at me. I'd see a car slow down for no reason
and feel my body tighten. Are they after me? I would be a big

catch for kidnappers—the foreigner, the American, the journalist—so I learned to keep my eyes and ears open.

It was a false sense of security. Other journalists, including Americans, were kidnapped and held for ransom. Other journalists, including two from CBS News, were killed while on assignment long after I left.

Not all my travel was this dangerous. There were the stories in Paris on the latest fashions, or in Wales covering the last remaining community choirs. The one constant was coming and going, sometimes with no more warning than a quick call home while I was hurrying to an airport.

I once joked with Jan that if either of us ever got the seven year itch, it would take fourteen years to develop, because I was gone half of the time.

I went when asked by the Bureau Chief, or the Foreign Editor, or the Executive Producer of this show or another. Jan always said she understood. She accepted what my job demanded, and this was one of the many reasons I could make her my life. I felt blessed, almost saved, when we fell in love, because my life before Jan was often a self-made horror.

I grew up a military brat, in a family always moving to the next assignment until I was in junior high school. My dad retired from the Army—he had been a pilot beginning in the days of World War Two—and we moved to the small town of Sidney in eastern Montana that boasted a population of 5,000 on a busy day. This was the town where my Danish immigrant grandfather had settled and farmed and where my father had grown up. My grandfather moved the family there in the 1920s because it already had a substantial Danish immigrant community and a Lutheran Church with services in Danish. Probably the only town in America where the Petersens, Hansens and Larsens far outnumbered the Smiths in the phone book.

When I was fifteen, I decided to become a journalist. It took two more years before someone paid me. The summer before entering college I got a job at the local weekly newspaper, the Sidney Herald. I quickly learned that the job wasn't about journalism, it was about grunt work. I swept up and helped with small printing jobs by stapling pages together. And to my great honor, once a week I washed the ink off the lead slugs in the flat page molds after the ancient press ran off a few thousand issues, wheezing and clanking all the way. If there is printer's ink in my blood, it seeped in the hard way. It took two or three days of steady washing to get that ink off my hands.

The good part happened when there was a breaking story and I got to cover it. One day it was a prairie fire west of town, and the editor let me race out with a notebook and a camera. I gave him a look so youthfully intense that I'm sure he smiled once I was out the door.

After graduation from the journalism school at Northwestern University, I went from being a newspaper reporter in Miami, Chicago, Omaha, and Milwaukee, to TV reporter in Milwaukee and then Minneapolis. My break was being hired by the Los Angeles Bureau of CBS News in 1978. I was the rookie correspondent, and that meant if a story developed in Portland at four on a Friday afternoon, I was the guy ready and eager to fly up and cover it. I would leave town at a moment's notice, which meant leaving my then-wife behind with shattered weekend plans . . . again. It didn't take long before she grew convinced that she was always going to be second best to a good feature story that might get on the Evening News.

It takes a combination of blindness and arrogance to destroy a marriage. I had both with my first. We made it through thirteen years, had two wonderful girls along the way, and made several lawyers richer in our angry parting.

This was the state of disrepair I called my life when I met Jan, and I didn't think I had a lot to offer. I was broke and sharing in the raising of two young children with an ex-wife. Not prime material for one's dating profile. But Jan didn't see it that way, and I decided that my best plan would be to prove her right.

In reality, we didn't have that much in common. Jan spoke French (fluently) and Italian (quite well), and I didn't. She studied European art history in college, and I studied journalism, American history and politics. She got good grades, I didn't. She was bubbly and charming and had a raft of friends. I was quiet and distrusted life too much to have many real friends. I think it was these differences that so attracted me to her. I relished taking care of her, and she felt safe in our love, that I would happily devote myself to making her happy.

And when she cared for me, the world melted into the background and I found my solace in her. I got the far better end of this bargain because I was the beneficiary of her enthusiasm for life and her spirit of adventure. She had other chances. There had been a first marriage, but it ended in disaster. She mentioned once that a rich Seattle lawyer wanted to marry her, but she turned him down. She wanted more, and I was it. I teased her about how she could have had an easier, somewhat more predictable and certainly more comfortable, life if she had married the lawyer. To which, of course, she laughed.

I worked to prove her right, and a way of doing that was creating special surprises for her. One year CBS brought us back from Moscow to New York so I could be the vacation fill-in anchor on the morning show news block. The stint crossed over September 1st, her birthday.

This was my chance to pay her back for all the things she did for me, like just loving me, which always seemed pretty amazing. I relished planning a special night for her because it meant thinking about the things she liked doing with me. This evening was going to be about sharing those things between us, so I arranged for dinner at the Rainbow Room on top of Rockefeller Center. We ate dinner and drank champagne while the city below glistened only for us. The orchestra played while I danced with her (badly) over and over.

When we got back to the hotel, I gave her the room key so she would be the one to open the door and see her next surprise. There in the center of the room was a round, metal statue from India, a Buddha of Many Hands. She had admired it when we were out shopping one day, so I snuck back and bought it for her. It was spiritual and mysterious, just like Jan. She loved it. I have it still, as a remembrance of making a wonderful evening that was a delight for both of us.

Celebrating life. She did it with such ease, and she let me build around her a place where her life could be celebrated across continents with experiences and adventures and where there was always one place of safety . . . and that place was in my love for her.

TIMELINE
January, 2006
Barry's update to family and friends

I know that Jan's e-mails are not terribly informative. You must simply accept this. She is rather vague about details these days, and she is hesitant about discussing her condition. I think that is understandable. All I can say is to keep sending her notes and I will keep encouraging her to answer them. If you have specific concerns that you want to discuss with me alone, send a note and I'll answer back.

At the moment, Jan is doing well. I can't guarantee how long that will go on, but I promise I'll do whatever I can to make it last.

Best from Tokyo.

~Barry

5

"Never shall I forget the days I spent with you. Continue to be my friend, as you will always find me yours."
~Ludwig van Beethoven

The Jan We Knew

I would like to believe that I made Jan feel loved every day. It wasn't something I would say just with words. There was always a quick hug or a kiss or a glance over the breakfast table so she could see in my eyes how much I loved her. And when she saw that, she smiled back. Better than words.

I always thought of her as "My Jan," but that wasn't altogether true. She shared that smile and that optimism with everyone who came into her world. As time passed, the loss of "Our Jan" became ever more apparent. Family, hers and mine, and friends, all began missing her spunk, tenderness, and quick sense of humor.

In an attempt to hold her close and provide comfort, people sent me notes and remembrances of their favorite stories. Little vignettes. Some were stories from the days before I knew her, which I love because they let me see her before there was "us."

Long before I met her, Jan worked at KIRO-TV in Seattle where she started in 1974. She was one of the first women reporters in the Seattle market. It wasn't too long before Annie Busch Marshall joined her in the newsroom. Annie wrote:

"I met Jan in September, 1979, when I came to work at KIRO-TV as a reporter/anchor. We were fast friends, the only two female faces on the air for an entire year. I had the day shift and Jan worked the night shift. Since it was still the early days of women in the newsroom or the work force for that matter, we were living in a man's world. We both worked to assert our sharp wits, determination and intelligence to make up for our gender and our height. We were both 5'2" tall, or more accurately, short.

"One day, the news consultant came to visit. He watched me anchor the Noon News and asked me why I didn't move around more on the set. He said I looked stiff. The answer was simple; my feet didn't touch the ground. I had to jack the chair up quite a bit to avoid looking too diminutive next to the much taller anchorman. So the station handyman built a box to put under my feet while anchoring. It was plywood, covered with carpet.

"Jan and I took this marvel of a box around the newsroom to get a new view on life and look a few people in the eye at a higher altitude. Jan especially enjoyed standing on the box and speaking with much taller males who preferred to brush off the 'little girls.' In fact, this added height brought her a new-found energy, and she had some rather pointed conversations. One guy became so uncomfortable with a taller, mightier Jan he told her step down from the box. Jan and I were quite amused by the entire scene.

"A few days later when Jan was trying to make her point about a story with a producer, she went to the set, picked up the box and proceeded to discuss her view while standing tall atop the box. She won."

I know the feeling of the guy who lost the argument. Jan was the Cute Blonde, but she held her ground well until she won. She was comfortable with who she was, what she believed, and how she wanted to live in this world. If she had a good idea, I quickly learned to adopt it because she was so often right.

Her confidence came from being the oldest, the one who had to watch out over the others when they were kids, and the one they looked up to . . . except when they thought she was pushy and called her "Bossy" without realizing that she considered that a compliment.

After Jan moved to San Francisco to be with me, we were often visited by her family. There were four younger brothers and sisters, and she was a superhero to the youngest, her brother, Dave.

"Jan was my 'big sister' with a nine year separation between us," Dave told me. He didn't have much time growing up with her; when Jan went off to college, he was still in elementary school.

When Dave was in college, he visited the Bay Area for a lacrosse tournament at Stanford University. Jan was working at the NBC station in San Francisco, and Dave was excited about coming up to visit—even if his appearance managed to scare nearly everyone who looked at him by the time he finally reached us. "I took a lacrosse stick to the mouth and received a lovely swollen and bloody lip that looked like an apricot hanging off my lip" he remembers, a tad painfully. "The night before going to see you and Jan in San Francisco I'd slept on the lawn of teammate's parents, so my hair was standing up on end. I hadn't showered after our games, and my lip was looking oh-so good.

"When I got to the TV station downtown, I'm sure the security guards thought I looked like someone down on his luck and who'd had spent the night living rough on the street. Luckily Jan came bouncing down the stairs, gave me a big hug and then laughed at my appearance.

"She gave me the keys to her car and directions to their house. After a long shower and a nap, we went to dinner, laughed way too much, and I was on a jet home the next day feeling very grown up having experienced San Francisco thanks to my big sister."

I wish Jan could remember this moment, when she made her little brother feel so grown up. She never stopped to consider that what she gave so naturally could mean so much to others. To her, this was just being a good sister and nothing unusual about that.

I envied that in her because that is something hard for me. She could give without the expectation of getting anything back in return, and I treasured her ease at being a great big sister, or a good friend, or a wife who loved me despite my many faults. She was a natural.

There were many times when she gave me that unquestioned love. She took it with us when we started our move from San Francisco to our first tour in Tokyo, and then on to Moscow. She joked that we had gone from Japan, a country in the 25th century, to Moscow still mired in about the 18th.

Part of that feeling was brought on by the gloom of Moscow. Lights were expensive and hard to come by, so only one out of every two or three streetlights worked. On a dark winter's night, the gloom spread wide. It was the same in people's homes. They would sit by the dimness of a single lamp because light bulbs were scarce.

So gloom was not something she would accept from me, especially on January 14, the day I turned forty. It was winter, cold and dark outside, which matched my mood. Turning a decade older, which was how I saw it, made me feel that I should have accomplished more in life. Or worse, that the best years were those already lived. I was busy moaning and looking in life's rear view mirror. All I wanted was to hide under the bedcovers and feel sorry for myself.

This was not for Jan. She decided the event wouldn't pass unnoticed or uncelebrated. Over our Christmas vacation in the US she secretly bought forty birthday greeting cards. All day long, despite my best efforts to ignore such a dreaded milestone, the cards popped up. On the breakfast table. In my coat pocket. In the bathroom, living room, bedroom. On my desk in the office. It finally had the desired effect. I forgot my gloom about aging and ended my endless conversations with anyone who would listen about being over the hill, and just laughed.

Jan had always been the one ready for a new adventure, the one ready to suggest a trip for us or with the girls and ready to laugh at me when I worried about the cost. But when we moved back for our second stint in Tokyo I noticed that Jan was changing. We didn't really realize why until she was finally diagnosed. Emily sent me this note remembering those days:

"We were going out to dinner one year at Christmas and I think we might have been trying a new restaurant. By then, it was unusual for us to go somewhere that Jan didn't already know well. Julie and I were getting ready, dressing up and wearing makeup we bought at the 100 Yen store (like the dollar stores in America), and Jan was supplementing any items we might have needed from her supply of makeup.

"As Julie and I stood facing the mirror, Jan coached us from behind while we applied our makeup. I remember her explaining all about how to do our eyes to make them look bigger, the way to put blush on your cheeks, and even some lipstick tutorials! It was one of those mother/daughter type moments, and it felt really good.

"At that point I think I already knew we weren't going to have Jan forever and so I treasured the happy moment."

"I'm sorry," Emily told me later when we talked about those times, "but remembering this makes me sad."

When we first left America for our overseas odyssey, we got homesick. So after a few years we scraped together some money and went to a place we loved, a development called the Sea Ranch. It's about three hours north of San Francisco by car with houses built along a ten-mile stretch of the Sonoma County coastline.

Whenever we could arrange a vacation there from the various places we lived, we would call up old friends from San Francisco to come up the coast and be with us, to walk the beach during the day, or sit in the hot tub and enjoy the starry nights.

John Carman and I worked together when I got a newspaper job fresh out of college, then we went our separate career ways. He later ended up in San Francisco as the TV critic for the San Francisco Chronicle, and we reconnected when CBS News moved me there. He was among the first to meet Jan when she moved to San Francisco to be with me, and he was among those we often invited to our Sea Ranch home. I had forgotten this little episode until John reminded me.

"I had a dog, a white standard poodle named Peabody, who occasionally had his own way to express his exhilaration about life: he bounced. It was close to a straight-legged vertical bounce -- boing! boing! boing!

"One weekend I drove Peabody up to your ocean side home in northern California. Peabody was a city dog. Sea Ranch promised new discoveries and sensory overload. I suppose I'd cleared Peabody first with you two, but I still worried you might privately harbor strong objections to a sizable and excitable dog in your home.

"From the moment we pulled into your driveway, Peabody was in doggy demon mode, boinging up and down around a brush area that surely reeked of deer scents and other exotic doggy delights.

"We entered the house. Peabody boinged through the doorway, skidded helter skelter across your brand new laminate floor, tumbled to an uncontrolled stop in front of his human hosts, and peed on the Pergo floor. I had one of those infinite moments of mortification. I looked at Jan, whom I knew to be a neatnik. On a detailed scale of unwanted introductions to my pet, this would occupy the penultimate rung.

"Jan threw her blonde head back and laughed. I think she laughed for about five minutes, or however long it took for my heart to resume its regular rhythm. Soon afterward, Peabody was back outside, boinging with abandon along the bluff overlooking the Pacific, at the back of your house. It seemed he might take one great, happy bounce over the bluff and into the ocean, but he managed to stay on land. As I recall, you and Jan watched and seemed to genuinely enjoy the show.

"It was Jan who set that tone and saved the day. What's a little puddle compared to such a striking demonstration of the simple joy of living?"

Walking Into Oblivion: Stage Four

A careful medical interview detects clear-cut deficiencies . . . decreased knowledge of recent occasions or current events; impaired ability to perform challenging mental arithmetic—for example, to count backward from 75 by 7s; decreased capacity to perform complex tasks, such as planning dinner for guests, paying bills and managing finances; reduced memory of personal history; the affected individual may seem subdued and withdrawn, especially in socially or mentally challenging situations. (Seven Stages of Alzheimer's Disease from www.alz.org, the Alzheimer's Association)

There was another slow but steady change . . . Jan was losing interest in meeting new people. When we moved back to Tokyo in 1995, the list of friends started out long, but in a few years ended at almost zero. Part of this was living overseas. Most journalists and business people are sent to a foreign posting for two or maybe three years. We made friends with other new journalists who, like us, had just moved to Tokyo.

Then they moved on, as did the neighbors in the apartment building who were our buddies. In two to three years almost all had left. But we stayed. As fresh faces showed up, it was harder for us to connect. We were not the new people dealing with a strange new place. We had dealt, thank you, and our interests had moved on. Our excitement quotient for exploring the usual first timer "must-see" temples and tourist sites was nil.

A few friends with a deeper investment in Japan stayed on for several years, yet in time they all finally left. It was a natural process. We were the odd ones for staying. And it seemed almost natural to run out of the energy needed for investing in new friendships. The next group of new arrivals, like the last, would just move away. Jan and I were not alone in this. Others who spent extended time overseas have had much the same experience.

And here is what I didn't want to see as it unfolded in front of me; Jan was a naturally outgoing and friendly person, well-liked by everyone around her. Yet despite that, she did not object or even react as our social life began to shrink. For a while, we lived next to the Tokyo American Club, a place with a gym, swimming pool, restaurants and numerous social groups. I asked Jan if she wanted to join the women's groups that sponsored day-trips. This would be an easy way to reach out and find new people who might become new friends.

No, she said, she wasn't interested. I accepted this and didn't push. After all, we were doing okay. I thought this was just us being self-sufficient, that we were enough for each other in life. I thought of it as an affirmation of our love.

In fact, it was not being self-sufficient at all. It was isolation closing in on us as Jan's brain ever so slowly closed down. Through these years we would return to the US to vacation at our home in northern California as often as we could. Jan loved being there.

And our friends there noticed, far sooner than I, that Jan's joy of being with other people had taken a slow and sad turn. Mary Alinder is the former assistant and biographer of Ansel Adams and one of the few people I know who considers the late chef and author Julia Child a personal inspiration, except that Mary can cook as creatively as Julia ever did. Dinners at her home are an event. Her husband, Jim, is a much-published photographer whose subjects vary greatly from panoramas of Paris to the landscape of California's north coast. The Alinder Gallery in Gualala, CA, sells fine, rare photographs, specializing in the work of Ansel Adams.

When I asked Mary and Jim what they saw in the last few years, this is what they shared:

"Jan defined the terms 'sparkling' and 'vivacious,' and she was certainly whip-crack smart, but she had never been one to dominate the conversation, rather adding a rare, appropriate comment that enriched that moment. Since we only saw you and Jan every few months when you came to your Sea Ranch home on vacation, one would think we could better sense the progress of her disease. Perhaps it was her radiant smile that fooled us for over a year. There came a time at one evening's end when we looked at each other and said, 'Did you hear what Jan said? It didn't make sense,' dismissing her off-the-wall remarks to mishearing.

"Her wonderful grin began to look pasted on. She spoke out with increasing rarity and sometimes what she uttered was spot on, but that became rarer, and her silences lengthened and deepened. She concentrated on the activity and banter about her with great focus, trying so desperately to hang on to the present and the reality of what was happening.

"It was an exhausting effort that lasted for shorter and shorter periods but she fought ferociously to be 'normal' for those times. We treasured those moments. We wish we had better honored her strength and determination, but we did not want to shatter the version of Jan that she heroically constructed so that she still could be one of us. The last time we saw Jan, she had become her own shadow."

6

"Passion and shame torment him, and rage is mingled with his grief."
~Virgil, a Roman poet

The Amateur Called to Caregiving

For the one who becomes the Alzheimer's caregiver, there is often no training, no manual, and no experience. Firefighters are taught how to handle a hose long before they are allowed close to the danger of the real thing. Doctors spend years in classes and hospitals learning to diagnose and heal. Even journalists, despite what many may believe, study, learn, and hone their craft. When someone is diagnosed with cancer, there are specialists and hospitals and machines to fight back. The experts take over.

Not with The Disease. On a Monday we are ordinary people doing our jobs, raising our families, and fretting over the mortgages or the kids. Then on a Tuesday, with no more warning than a doctor's diagnosis, we are recruited, without asking, into a job for which we have no preparation and facing sudden downward changes in our lives that we cannot predict.

Save for the rare person who might have some medical training, the rest of us are amateurs in this new calling; ordinary people whose sole qualifications are geography and love—we are the nearest and dearest to the person with The Disease.

And we are many; an estimated ten million people are unpaid caregivers for those five million with Alzheimer's. Were we paid, says a study by the Alzheimer's Association, we would have earned about $94 billion for our time and effort. And when the number of Alzheimer's sufferers triples to an estimated sixteen million by about 2050, the number of unpaid caregivers will hit 32 million.

Add it up . . . almost fifty million people will be overcome by this disease. So many, in fact, that you will surely know someone, or your family will include one. Or you may be the one with the diagnosis, or with the caregiver's responsibility. Such are the odds.

My attempt at mastering this new profession unfolded in three acts. The first act was taking care of Jan by myself. The second was hiring a live-in caregiver. The third was moving her into an assisted living facility in the United States — on the other side of the Pacific Ocean from our life in Asia. The first almost cost me my job, the second almost cost me my health, and the third all but ended my sanity.

In our first years together, Jan and I were partners in everyday life. She and I both worked and earned money. I focused on the job with the full-time salary, and she worked part-time and did all of the things, like paying the bills, which kept our household running. She made dinner, and I bought wine on the way home.

Life is a series of ordinary moments shared, and the pleasure is in that sharing. We talked endlessly, planning things such as where to make a real estate investment or whom to call for a dinner date. Sometimes the evening conversation was just one of us letting off steam from a bad day. Sharing it made it easier.

We went to bed contented, knowing that we would wake up and make coffee and have breakfast and start another day sharing our lives. There was a solace in that, a trust that as long as we were together we could shield each other from the worst the world outside could inflict. Being together was the core of our strength. The Disease attacked the core. That's what it does. That is its strategy.

And one of its main targets is the frontal lobes of the brain.

The frontal lobes are considered our emotional control center and home to our personality. There is no other part of the brain where lesions (an injury to the brain, in this case caused by the disease) can cause such a wide variety of symptom . . . The frontal lobes are involved in motor function, problem solving, spontaneity, memory, language, initiation, judgment, impulse control, and social and sexual behavior. (Courtesy of the website for the Center for Neuro Skills - www.neuroskills.com/tbi/bfrontal.shtml)

The diagnosis brought focus to what I was seeing. I knew
The Disease would change us, but how? And how much? As a
person who loves history, the first months after the diagnosis
brought a moment of world history to mind. In September, 1939,
the Germans invaded Poland triggering declarations of war.
European alliances were forged, weapons were manufactured
and sides chosen . . . but there was no major fighting.

The British called these months the "Phony War," an
uneasy period that lasted until May of 1940, when German
troops marched into Belgium, the Netherlands, and Luxembourg
and the fighting was suddenly, and terribly, on.

In that brief calm, no one could imagine how devastating
World War II would become . . . beautiful and vibrant cities
bombed to ruins, the unspeakable concentration camps,
developing and dropping the atomic bomb. Instead, in that brief
period, life went on as before, and one could almost hope that
maybe what Winston Churchill called "The Gathering Storm,"
would go away.

It was like that for me, a hope that grew as the shock of the
diagnosis sank into an uneasy calm when nothing dramatic
happened right away. This was the true beginning of denial, and
I deluded myself into thinking that maybe I'd overestimated
how bad this would be, so ordinary were those first immediate
months.

Jan could do all the things she had done before the
diagnosis . . . go to the grocery store in Tokyo, work out in the
gym if we were at the hotel in Beijing. She went out of the
apartments less in both cities, of course, and I called home a bit
more often checking up on her. But there was a sense of
normalcy, of life going on as before.

We had dinner when I wasn't traveling. We'd talk about the
day before going into the other room to watch a movie—
preferably a comedy since I wanted every evening to be upbeat.
Life continued in a soothing way even though it was a constantly
altering rhythm as she slipped a touch here or there. I would
notice it, she wouldn't. I kept it to myself and adjusted.

I found myself making more and more decisions, and
eventually I was making every decision for both of us, from
organizing the next three-city visit to see family and friends in

the US, to what we both might have as the main course for dinner. Also ending was the shared responsibilities for keeping the house going. Our bank account swelled for a few months and I couldn't figure out why until the Tokyo landlord called and said Jan hadn't paid the rent for three months. I took over the checkbook and paid all the bills. Another shifted responsibility.

We put great faith in medicine in this day and age, and Jan decided that the pills and a positive attitude made the difference. I arranged for the pills, and the positive attitude flowed from deep within her spirit.

The first medication stalled The Disease for a while. When The Disease started making new inroads, we switched to another pill. Once again, it slowed the progression and for a while brought parts of Jan back. I schooled myself about the existing medications and was disheartened at their limitations. Depending on the patient, they only work for a while, if at all. In the beginning I was hypersensitive to stories about trials of new experimental medications. But like everything else about The Disease, the trials ended with failure after failure, and my interest and hope faded for a new breakthrough.

At first, I drew my ammunition from Jan's inborn optimism. If she believed we could beat The Disease, then I intended to believe with her, and it made me feel better. Sure, there were studies and terrifying statistics about Early Onset Alzheimer's Disease and how it caused dramatically shorter life spans. Alzheimer's can kill in anywhere from three to twenty years.

But Jan and I were determined not to be just another statistic. And with help from the pills, there were times when it almost felt like we were indeed winning, which I defined as keeping The Disease at bay. We wanted a cure, but we would settle for just freezing the deterioration so she could live out the rest of her life where she was. Frankly, we would settle for anything positive.

Reading about Alzheimer's also meant learning about caregiver stress, and how caregivers often die before the person with The Disease. I shrugged this off, thinking that this kind of mortality was more about elderly couples, about the eighty-year-old overwhelmed wife who dies from the stress and exhaustion of caring for her eighty-year-old husband. What I forgot was that caregiving was a new job that starts out feeling part-time and then grows to consume every hour you have, day and night, 24/7.

And like so many other Early Onset caregivers, I already had a day job that needed doing, and it was the one that paid my salary. I was on call day or night if a broadcast needed a story. Since Asia is on almost opposite time zones from New York, it meant that I had to get up at midnight or 2 a.m. to return to the office and write a script if someone in New York needed something. And if we were covering a breaking story, it usually meant I would stay up through most of the night, grab what hours of sleep I could, and keep going.

In 1997, we rushed to Guam to cover the story about a Korean Airlines 747 that slammed into a hillside on approach to the airport. I put in more than eighty hours straight without sleep, doing stories for the morning show, the Evening News, radio, and even a piece for *48-Hours*. But it wasn't only the stories that needed to be covered. With cutbacks in network news, my Asia job was harder than ever. When I was first posted in Tokyo in 1986, there were four CBS News correspondents and bureaus in Asia: Tokyo, Beijing, Hong Kong and Bangkok. When I came back in 1995, Hong Kong, and Bangkok were long since closed, and the office in Beijing now consisted of just a camera crew. From four correspondents, we were down to one. Me.

I knew it would be more challenging, and I talked with Jan before we decided on the move. We both felt this was an opportunity for me to cover stories that were done by other correspondents last time around. It could also mean more time away from home.

For her, it was a fair tradeoff. Maybe I'd be on a few more airplanes, but those airplanes were not taking me to Sarajevo or Baghdad. Jan would happily exchange a few more nights alone with me on the road someplace in Asia for those nights of fear knowing I was someplace where I could get hurt . . . or worse.

In 2002 the job took on a new demand. Until then I was based primarily in Tokyo, but the Chinese insisted that we pay more attention to China or lose our journalist accreditation. So

CBS rented a serviced one-bedroom furnished apartment in Beijing, and Jan and I started a two-city life. I would be in Beijing anywhere from a week to months at a time, depending on stories that needed doing, and usually with little or no warning about when we needed to change cities.

And like any foreign correspondent, when I went to work in Tokyo or Beijing in the morning, I had no way of knowing in what city or country I would be sleeping that night. An earthquake, a plane crash, a story that caught some executive producer's eye drove my professional life. I carried a passport with me everywhere because sometimes the call would come and there was barely enough time to get to the airport. I was expected and paid for making it onto that flight and to that story.

The time away from Jan could be a few days. But when I was sent to Pakistan in late 2001 and ended up covering the kidnapping of Wall Street Journal reporter Daniel Pearl, the assignment stretched into two months. Pearl was executed by his kidnappers in Karachi, Pakistan, on February 1, 2002.

I wanted to make it up to her, to thank her for being home by herself and living on phone calls from me and not on the touch and holding that we both craved from each other. And I needed to somehow reassure her that I was okay, even after covering the story of another journalist who was, in the end, murdered. We needed time alone to celebrate being alive.

I called our travel agent and booked her on a plane to Paris where I met her. We walked and shopped and ate at wonderful restaurants, as we had the first time we went during the first months of our marriage. This was before the formal diagnosis, before everything was colored by The Disease, and that is why it is such a good and fond memory for me.

But even being home offered no real respite from the growing demands of work. The pressure to get on the air never ended, especially in Tokyo. A high level of story production was the only way we could justify the expense of a bureau in one of the world's most expensive cities. I felt that the jobs of the others in the office—the field producer, the Japanese staff, the cameraman, the editor—rested, in large part, in my hands. If the producer and I came up with stories that were getting on the air, we made everyone look good. If the story count slipped, questions from the home office would naturally follow; why was the company spending a lot and getting back only a little. More than ever, it was critical to keep ourselves looking good.

It essentially meant my day never ended. If there was a good story on a Sunday, then we damn well wanted to get on the air, so we worked on Sunday. They call journalism the first draft of history. I would go, see events, talk to people, and then condense it into an *Evening News* report.

One Sunday morning, about 1 a.m., I got called into the office to write a story concerning Asia, but when I got there I was unable to focus, unable to draw together the various facts needed for the script, or organize in my mind the video that was available for me to use in the story. This was my job, and I'd failed. I was on the phone with the executive producer, an old friend, and I started crying and saying that I just didn't have the energy. I was simply exhausted. I didn't see it then, and wouldn't for a long time, but this was the first symptom of the toll that being a caretaker was taking on me. What fool thinks he can do it all, the work and the caregiving, when neither really end? That fool was . . . me.

The producer in New York who wanted the story that night was understanding and gracious and said the story wasn't that important. She told me to go home and try to sleep.

But rather than going home, I curled up on the floor and fell asleep next to the phone, in case she changed her mind. The incident shook me. How had I come to this? As I lay on the floor, I wondered what my bosses would think if they heard about this night. Wasn't this dangerous behavior if I wanted to keep working? One simple answer was that they would think I could no longer do my job. This would not end well for me.

It didn't take middle of the night calls to wear me out. Caregiving was doing that just fine, thanks. One morning a colleague walked into my office and asked the casual, "How are you?"

"I'm tired," I answered.

"You're always tired," she said in response. I thought about her comment and realized she was right. I did always feel tired. It was the mental tiredness from having one part of my brain constantly attuned to Jan; how she was doing, where she was, was she okay.

And most of all, would I be home that night to care for her, or would I be off somewhere on a story? In years past, that wasn't a problem. It was work, and Jan accepted it. But this was not about her approval. If I wasn't there, would she remember to take her pills in the morning, or would she go for a walk somewhere and forget where she was. Or worse, would she try and cook something and then go take a nap and forget the stove was on.

This loop of questions and worry ran loud in my head, and I dared not turn it down. She needed a caregiver with never ending vigilance, and I wanted to be that caregiver because I loved her. But the reality, ever slow to dawn on me, was that I may not be the most dependable person for this job because of all the traveling I had to do. The pressure was building, and so was the exhaustion. It took covering a story away from home for me to discover my journey was the road to destruction.

The question was always the same for me: How do you fight back against a disease you can't beat? I found a way—I took it out on the rest of the world, and got to know a new emotion one-on-one—uncontrollable rage. It began deep in my stomach, a welling up until my gut hurt, and the adrenaline poured into my system.

I could feel it taking over my body, starting with my stomach tightening. Some part of my brain would try and stop the emotions, sending warnings that this was not good, that I was losing control. I got good at ignoring those warnings.

Instead, I would feel it in my whole body. To others it seemed like a spilling of anger, but from the inside there was the rage that The Disease attacked Jan. She was an innocent; she was someone who brought smiles into other people's lives.

The rage took over because I could simply not hold it in, and maybe, in part, because I wanted it out, yearning for some searing catharsis, even if it was about losing control around others.

I couldn't aim my anger at Jan, even though the anger was all about The Disease and what it was doing to her. So it erupted at odd times and toward people who had no warning of what was coming, and no understanding about what had triggered my outburst. Someone made a small mistake or irritated me, and I exploded into a screaming, irrational rage.

One day, in southern China, we were outside about to shoot a key interview. It was a lovely day and we had just finished lunch, courtesy of our hosts. The translator was standing with me, the cameraman behind me, the sound man on the other side, and the producer was behind monitoring the questions and the shot. As I asked the first question, the cameraman stopped me. The eye contact was wrong because the person was looking at the translator and not at me. We asked him to look at me.

I started again. The sound man stopped me. There was a problem with the audio. I blew up. I screamed and lashed out with a rash of obscenities. Get it damn right, what kind of professionals are you, I can't focus if you keep interrupting me, can't you do your jobs?

Then, with much effort, I tamped down the rage, and we started again. Later, as we drove away, I fumbled out an apology. Stress, maybe I hadn't slept that well. Frankly, whatever I said was lame. What could I tell them? My life is now all about rage?

The people with whom I worked became wary around me, cautious lest I blow up over something. And they had no idea what it would be next. I didn't blame them. Even I became wary around me. The rage was so easily triggered because it had no real target, and there was never absolution. I couldn't be angry with Jan. She didn't cause this. What use was it to be angry with God? I couldn't call Him out and have a decent fistfight, and punish Him for what he'd done to my Jan, who didn't deserve this. How could I ever exorcise this rage from my system?

Like most caregivers, I thought I was alone. It wasn't until I got a note from a friend whose wife was also slipping away from Early Onset Alzheimer's and was relieved to find another person caught up these emotions. There was kinship in that. Rage, it seemed, was contagious. I wasn't alone after all. Part of his note:

"We continue to slide slowly downhill—she in her ability to speak and do even the simplest of chores, me in my ability to control my temper. I never turn it on her, but all it takes is a broken shoe lace, and I go ballistic."

When I was on the road, there was the unending worry about making sure she was safe. Especially with cooking or, more precisely, using the stove. Cooking had always been her therapy, and it hurt to think about taking this away from her. In the old days, before she got sick, I remember how she wanted to teach me how to cook, so sure she was that I would be able to learn. I would laugh and tell her that she was such a master, it was like Picasso telling Mrs. Picasso that he could teach her how to paint, it being so easy and all for him.

She was still shopping and cooking for us when we were in Tokyo, and I considered that a good sign. But there were more occasions when she brought dinner to the table and left the stovetop burner on high heat. I got into the habit of checking the burners, which I then considered problem solved. But what about when I was on the road? Simple. I would just call and ask about the stove. Problem solved. But, of course, it was only solved in my mind because she could have hung up the phone and headed straight for the stove. It would not occur to her to tell me that the stove was on.

When I told people about Jan's diagnosis, I saw fear in their eyes, the fear of the words "Alzheimer's Disease." There is a natural, human terror of The Disease. Other illnesses may take away some of our abilities, and the effects of other diseases can often be seen. Not The Disease. It takes what we have all had since birth, the mind and its memories, and our ability to talk, dream, and imagine. I cannot fathom what it is like, even now, except the raw fear that it will happen to me.

And when we see the person who looks as Jan does, still beautiful and bubbly, we want to reject that she is ill in any way.

I know this rejection well because I did exactly the same thing. I would delude myself with daydreams that there might, one day, be another moment as defining as the moment when I knew we would always be together. In my daydream, Jan would suddenly get well after some miraculous medical advance, and then this nightmare would end. And (in this improbable, but constant, daydream) after this miracle took place we would laugh about the fear and how the bad days were behind us, all the while sipping champagne to celebrate her wellness. We would pick up our lives and all would be back to normal.

Wouldn't someone invent a vaccine, a shot that would bring her back? It had to happen soon, because the truth of where she was going couldn't be happening to us. My mind screamed in denial. I could not allow this.

The screaming didn't matter. The rage didn't have any effect. The daydreams were useless, or worse, they fed my ongoing denial. The changes came when The Disease decided, not me. My daughters tried helping me in this new job as caregiver on those times when we were all together. Sometimes it was heartbreaking.

We all met in Palm Springs, CA for Christmas in 2006. I rented a house with a pool and a mass of bedrooms. Emily and her husband Craig drove from Denver with their dog, and Julie flew in a few days later. We goofed off, sat by the pool, and read books, or napped, and shopped for silly Christmas decorations.

I bought presents for everyone from "Dad and Jan," but I knew Jan had no presents for me, because I had done all our packing for the trip. The girls and I hatched a plan, and we went to a book store and I picked out two or three truly trashy mystery novels, suitable for long airplane flights, and the store wrapped them in bright Christmas paper. The plan was that the girls would slip the books to Jan and she could slide them under the delightfully garish 2-foot high revolving plastic electric Christmas tree and feel that she was gift-giving to me.

She wouldn't do it. Flat out, not interested. Somehow, she had it fixed in her mind that my Christmas present was going to be a new suit by Armani—that is what Barry needed and deserved, she said. The practical reality was that there was no way we were going to go suit shopping. I was overweight and didn't want to spend the money on an expensive suit, especially as the credit card bills soared from our vacation.

No matter . . . forget any books for Barry, the present from her would be a suit and if she couldn't get it just then, she would buy it later. And that became her present of choice for Christmas and my birthdays from then on. The Armani suit was a fixation for her, the perfect present for Barry that she would pick out, if not now, later.

Later never came.

TIMELINE
Summer, 2007
Barry's update to family and friends

We were back in the US in June and saw Jan's neurologist in San Francisco. During these appointments the doctor administers a quick test where she memorizes a few items, writes sentences, gives the day and date, what city she is in, etc.

It was clear that Jan was having a lot of trouble with short-term memory. For instance, given a list of five items, she could not remember any of them about two minutes later. This was a significant difference from our last visit.

COMPENSATING: This is a new one, and I am told it is not unusual at this point. I noticed Jan reacting to my questions with answers that showed she couldn't remember something but didn't want to admit it.

Jan is "compensating" in other ways. The other day she went shopping at the local "Friendship Store" (a store in Beijing where we lived part time while in Asia) which sells Chinese goods to tourists. Jan wrote "Friendship Store" on her wrist. When I asked that night where she went, she flipped over her wrist and had the answer ready.

I also noticed something else unusual for Jan; she closed herself off to new experiences. This happened when someone suggested that she might enjoy visiting a local produce market. She got visibly angry. A little research shows that this is probably not anger, but fear. It can be daunting to contemplate doing new things. This was noticeable because Jan was usually first in line for new experiences.

I must confess that I am taken aback at how fast Jan's short term memory seemed to evaporate . . . it robs us of sharing daily experiences, and robs her of savoring the good things that are a part of all of our daily lives.

This is hard for me because I find that I can no longer have long conversations about complicated things. She doesn't really follow me that well. She'll hear a word or phrase and suddenly head the conversation off in a different direction.

I am losing more than a friend . . . also slipping away is the one person who was my confidante, with whom I could and did share everything.

I feel like I'm trapped in a movie, watching it unfold and already knowing the ending . . . but with no way to rewind back to the good parts.

~Barry

7

"If a situation requires undivided attention, it will occur simultaneously with a compelling distraction."
~Hutchinson's Law

The Disease Takes Me for a Ride

People who spend time with me, and who are foolish enough to ask, will find that I have a passion about cars from the 1950s. It goes back to being a boy in the '50s who, at age seven or eight years old, could sit next to my dad in the front seat of our two-toned cream and green Mercury sedan driving down a highway and tell him the names of the cars coming at us by shape and design. "Buick" I would say, noting the distinctive front end, and do exactly the same for "Chrysler" or "Ford."

There were times when I could tell the model and year. "Last year's Plymouth," I would bark out with childlike confidence. "The cheaper model." I grew out of this in the 1960s when cars got bigger and bulkier and, to my changing taste, not as interesting as something called girls.

When my daughter, Julie, graduated with honors in chemistry from college and was going on to graduate school on a full-ride scholarship, I told her I would buy her a car and suggested a little Mercedes two-seater from the 1970s, or maybe a classic 1966 Mustang convertible? They were really quite reasonable and easy to maintain.

"Dad," she said evenly, with the tone of voice children use when they need to reign in their straying parents. "I don't want a car that is older than I am." I got her a Volkswagen. New.

Imagine the pure joy when the internet came along with eBay and its whole section on "collector" cars for sale. It was like being back in my childhood, spending hours looking, analyzing, imagining what it would be like to drive that 1950s Cadillac or the over-the-top Chrysler with tail fins so high they would reach to my chest. I didn't get a driver's license until 1965, long past the era when these cars had ruled the highway. By 1965, they were retired to junk yards or scrap heaps. Imagine, I would think.

Therapists call it retail therapy and say we shop and buy as a way of avoiding pain. More precisely, maybe I did it to avoid life. I would describe it as my shopping anti-depression therapy: buying something will cheer us up.

That may have been part of it. And just as surely, distraction from The Disease was part of it. Distraction helped me ignore the financial unsoundness of this. I told myself a lie, one of many in those days, that old cars would become more valuable as time goes on. The truth is that a few do, but most don't. And mine surely didn't.

This was a sign of how The Disease was changing me. I started buying old cars because I had some extra money, a cushion that could be critically vital later on in caring for Jan. But I didn't see ahead to "later." I saw right now and I wanted something right now.

The first car I bought remains my favorite. And, as The Disease grew to dominate our lives and bank account and finances, it was the first to be sold because it was the easiest to sell, the one that would not linger on the showroom floor of a collector car dealer. It was a Titian-red 1960 Buick Electra 225 convertible with, true to the era, leather bucket seats. The '225' actually had a meaning—the number of inches the car was long. It came out to almost nineteen feet. I used to joke that it was so big it could qualify for its own zip code. It wouldn't fit in many modern-day garages.

Jan and I loved that car. We kept it at our house in northern California in a garage-sized storage locker and had a friend take it on regular drives to keep it running when we were gone. And when we were there on vacation . . . my goodness! You knew the Petersens were in town because we would swoop down two-lane Highway One along the California coast in this nineteen-foot red convertible with tail fins and the top down. The top always had to be down, that was unbroken protocol.

I would make an exception for a heavy torrential downpour and put the top up, but your average dense fog or light to medium sprinkles (known as rain) was something to be embraced for the sheer joy of feeling the wind (and water) blowing through your hair (or matting it to your soaking head). It was the owning of an experience that we could have with just the twist of a key.

The car craziness should have stopped there, but it didn't. I became addicted to surfing collector cars for sale on eBay. I subscribed to magazines specializing in collector cars. I found web sites with extensive histories of these cars, written with surprising affection by others similarly smitten by Detroit's style evolution as the '50s and '60s unfolded and America's prosperity and car sizes soared.

First were the bulky early '50s models, then came the mid-decade space age influence with cars actually named things like Rocket 88. And there were the streamlined jet-fighter tail-fins with models competing over which had the highest, longest fins and then all of that suddenly evaporating in the '60s when fins disappeared and style took second place to sheer bulk. Want a nineteen-foot car? Well step this way, sir, because we now have several monster models.

I bought a second collector car, an Oldsmobile Starfire, which my son-in-law fixed up. So far, so good. We sold it and made a modest profit, justifying my new-found shopping therapy. But why the third? Then the fourth. Click, click, just add more money to the eBay bid. And on it went, until the fleet numbered seven. Most were cars selling for less than a second-hand old Ford or Subaru. But a couple took a big chunk of my money.

And they were scattered . . . a Thunderbird roadster convertible bought in Illinois I had shipped to Arizona where someone was going to re-build the engine. A Chrysler Imperial bought in California also moved to Arizona to be stored by friends. I bought a 1953 Buick Skylark in Denver and had it shipped to Illinois to a restoration expert who dealt exclusively with early 1950s Buicks. It was beaten up and slightly rusted. I bought a beast and thought, well, someday, it will be a beauty. The reality that restoring it to be a pristine piece of American automotive sculpture would cost more than the car might ever be worth was something to think about . . . later . . . if then.

A 1958 Cadillac Eldorado Biarritz convertible was shipped to one of the country's best 1950s Cadillac restoration companies, located in upper New York State. Just the name—Biarritz—was enough to blind me. A Cadillac! A convertible! The '50s! The fact that it needed a paint job, the engine rebuilt, a whole new interior and don't even talk about the transmission and brakes, that was tomorrow's worry.

The retail therapy included not just shopping but researching the background of each potential purchase by talking with the owner or the mechanic who cared for it, and then checking its value against books and websites that specialize in collector car prices.

Then figuring out where to have the car moved and what company would pick it up here and deliver it there. It meant late night phone calls and wire-transferring money and it was amazingly . . . and this was the point . . . consuming in its attention to detail.

Somehow, in my mind, having these cars let me feel like I was a strutting teenager in slicked back hair, wearing a t-shirt with a pack of Camels rolled up in the sleeve. Cool. Elvis cool. I had the cars to prove it.

This image, by the way, had nothing to do with my high school years when I was a classic nerd in big glasses who never, ever wore a t-shirt to school or anywhere else. And while people would have described me in many ways during high school, cool was not one of them.

If this doesn't seem silly enough, then consider that I lived in Asia and could not drive these cars which were scattered across the US, and some didn't even work. With the exception of the red Buick Electra 225, these were cars I had others test drive and then had the cars moved by transport companies. There was no daily driving pleasure in this for me. The pleasure of driving them (I told myself) would surely come later. Unless, as happened once or twice, I sold one and bought another and the cycle would churn on.

To put it another way, to be clear about this, I was in a world of self-delusion. I spent money and then committed to spending more money for repairs or storage, while lying to myself by saying that this was okay because it was a good financial investment.

And for this I had a willing, encouraging and unwitting partner; Jan. On a Sunday afternoon I might go hunting for her in the apartment to come back to the den and see what I had found on the computer.

"Look at this," I would say proudly. "It's a 1957 Thunderbird in great shape."

"It's beautiful," she would say, her voice matching my enthusiasm, sitting down in a nearby chair, folding her hands in her lap, leaning forward and giving the car on the computer screen her full attention.

"What do you think, darling? Should we get it? Would you like riding in this one?"

"Sure, if YOU like it!" was her happy answer. And just as she would repeat thoughts and sentences, she would repeat this line to me: "Sure, if YOU like it!" Her cheery tone would mimic my boyhood enthusiasm.

Without meaning to, and certainly without knowing it, she was enabling me. I listened to her giving me permission and I heard only the part I wanted to hear . . . not the impaired judgment of someone with a brain-altering disease, but the words pure and permissive: Sure, if YOU like it!

We would talk about cars over lunch or dinner, how we could use this car or that car, whichever one I was in love with that day, and I could babble endlessly about what it could be worth with a new interior or paint job. I could spend distracted hours on the web with a mission, learning about a car I might want to buy, understanding its history. Was it prone to rust? Were parts readily available? What did people say about how it handled in today's high-speed freeway traffic?

Jan wants the car (she said so herself, "Sure, if YOU like it!") so there was her encouragement. Why not spend the once carefully hoarded money? Wouldn't this be something we would share, cruising together in our cool cars?

Why worry about some Alzheimer's induced far-away rainy day when there were already thunderstorms and tornadoes and hailstones raking across my life right now. I found temporary shelter in distraction.

This was not me, the person who always considered himself a careful investor. The first house I bought, and the second and the third, I re-sold myself, each in a different state. I learned each state's real estate rules, bought ads in the newspaper and put up colorful flags and held an open house on Sundays. I showed the house myself because I wanted to pocket the profit, not share it with a real estate agent. The money made from one house was carefully rolled over into the next one, since I kept a wary eye on the tax laws about real estate. I was happy to put in the hours marketing the house myself for the reward and delighted to take the money to buy something else that I could improve and make another profit.

There was a time early in my working life when I bought new cars, but that ended because I couldn't stand the depreciation on a new car. So I bought used cars instead. Doing that meant money saved, and wisely. When 401Ks came along, I signed up for the max. If there was an IRA that Jan or I qualified for, we funded it to the limit. Money in savings or investments tucked away for the future was money we could not spend now.

I was a mutual fund, long-term bond kind of guy. That was how I slept well at night. When my first daughter was born, my financial reaction was to buy life insurance to make sure my budding new family would always be cared for.

Alzheimer's starts small with the caregiver being a bit more careful about the well being of the person with The Disease. Then the caregiving demands escalate, and some people must give up their jobs and income because of those demands. Then come the expenses for part-time or full-time caregivers, or for moving into assisted living facilities. It ends at the single most expensive point of needing full-time care when the person with Alzheimer's slides into a vegetative state.

The odd thing is that I knew what was coming. This journey may move at its own pace with each different person, but the end of the road is well-marked and well-known. All my life I saved and planned and worried about providing for a financially easy future. I did that until The Disease spread its gloom over me and I needed some point of light, some excitement, some exhilaration giving me gratification now.

Why, I ask myself now, did I do this when the financially conservative thoughtful side of my brain, the side that had spent decades building a diversified nest egg, was screaming for attention with arms waving wildly? Oh nuts, said the other side of the brain, just shut up! This is about fun. I deserve this. Retail therapy has the deadening effect on pain by buying something. But it went beyond that.

It also helped deaden the sense of loss as Jan was changing. My mind could focus instead on the details of a 1950s car engine rebuild cost and not have to be whirling day and night with grief or anger about there being less of Jan here today than yesterday or last week. And it was also a way to not think about a future that was now a darkening, deepening shadow. Instead, buy another something with shiny paint and chrome. Pretend and distract, using a distorted financial logic (the more I spend, the more I will somehow reap) that could just as easily prove summer will never end and winter will never come if you just wish it that way.

Wishing would not make The Disease go away. But maybe I could chase it into a corner, push it off a small distance, or just get it out of my consciousness and allow me something else to think about. And when expenses started mounting, and it was inevitably time to start selling the cars, I chose the one I loved best, the Titian-red 1960 Buick convertible. The one I thrilled in driving, the one that Jan loved being in. The one that held our California Highway One memories.

I wondered later why I chose that particular one as the first to go, and the answer is guilt. Who was I to enjoy and have the thrill of driving this lovely car when Jan was ill? And how could I ever get into that car again without her at my side, her head slightly back as the wind rushed through her blond hair. As long as I had that car, I would have her ghost with me every time I sat behind the wheel. I'd no longer enjoy the distraction or feel the excitement when the engine came alive at my touch, but rather the emptiness and missing her next to me, and finally the rage about days that were not meant to end. The car I loved would become something to hate.

And if I gave up the one possession that represented so much fun, the car that exhilarated me like that kid from the '50s, would that somehow cauterize the ache of failure I felt for not somehow protecting Jan from this disease?

In truth, it was just a car . . . an engine, four tires, a steering wheel. But for me it was the boyhood fascination, my touching and rubbing it like a piece of sculpture. Or feeling a pulsing excitement at how its monster V-8 hummed as I steered it down the road and people who saw it waved in appreciation and I waved back, being Mr. Cool.

So selling this car was also a way to inflict injury on myself. Jan was losing something, so I deserved to feel pain as well. And as Jan slid ever further away, anything that brought pleasure was too selfish and had to be clawed out of life. Starting with the cool-car dream I loved the most. Because it seemed that all the dreams were ending.

TIMELINE
Summer, 2007
E-mail from Dick Lundgren, whose wife, Dorothee, also has Early Onset Alzheimer's Disease:

I know only too well the feeling of being alone. We are slowly losing our best friend, even though they are still physically here with us. They are not and will never again be the person we married.

The loneliness we feel is our grieving for the loss of that person. We are also in the process of going from being a spouse to being a parent. I feel as though I am 90% to 95% parent to Dorothee today.

All aspects of being married have mostly disappeared. Our sex life died months ago and even giving her a hug is difficult because she doesn't seem to understand. The way I kiss her anymore is on the cheek.

~Dick

8

"So, fall asleep love, loved by me . . . .for I know love, I am loved by thee."
~Robert Browning

The Beginning of Endings

Could I have been so naïve? So worldly in the good and evil ways of man and yet, so blind to how The Disease would silently slide between us and destroy our coming together. There was logic to not believing.

Alzheimer's often attacks the frontal lobe of the brain, and the desire for sex must come from some more primal part of the brain. At least that's how I would have explained it had someone asked me. But no one asked, and no one warned me that this, too, was a sacrifice that The Disease would not demand or discuss. It would just take.

We were blessed with being two people who couldn't keep their hands off each other. We would touch and hold and kiss just because we passed each other in the kitchen. Jan was beautiful, a true five-foot-two blonde, pin-up curvy. She was sensual and spirited, and made it very clear she wanted me, just me. Such are these blessed things when you are a man, a husband, and a lover.

Our lovemaking was sometimes slow and easy and sometimes quick and instant, as I sought for her release that left her satisfied and the more hungry for me, and me for her. And then we would find in each other the chance to be as one, to hold each other and feel that these two bodies could, if only for that instant, share one soul.

I don't know when it changed, not the year or the feeling. It crept in, unspoken, un-thought. Do we not all have moments when our lover, our dearest friend, feels ever so slightly distant? Distracted? But the distance didn't go away. Sometimes it felt like I had beaten it back a little, had gotten through to her. Sometimes . . . not.

At first I blamed myself, and that was okay. I could do it better, find something more creative. I read books and articles looking for ideas and then tried them. It didn't work. That is when I realized that we were losing our intimacy. What God had joined together, The Disease was putting asunder. And thus began a whole new descent for me, driven by knowing this was another something that I could neither control nor change.

It wasn't just loneliness; it was an enforced, unwanted isolation. Our lovemaking had always been a strong connection, as it is between any two people who love each other. Without it, I began feeling adrift and confused over what to do about this. I never expected to feel alone when I was with Jan, but now I did even with her beside me because I was without this connection, this closeness, the moments that made the two of us into one.

And what about Jan? Did she understand what The Disease was doing, how it was forcing us apart . . . how she was going away and how scared that made us both feel?

She knew. I'm sure of it. Not with words, necessarily, but with her instinct and her eyes. She knew it the time we were tangled and locked together and I looked down at her and was stunned to see her eyes wide open, staring hard and unblinking at me. Not with passion or pleasure, but as if she was trying to freeze this exact moment in her mind—that if she stared hard enough and long enough she could remember this moment a day or just an hour from now.

I gathered her in my arms and told her how much I loved her, and then held her long after there was nothing left to say. I stayed that way until she found comfort in sleep. There were still occasional times when I could touch her and the woman inside would find her hunger for me, and we would be together, the way I once believed would never end. But it was ending.

Is this too much to share, to know about Early Onset Alzheimer's? But there is more.

As The Disease progressed, she became more unsure of herself and more dependant on me to make almost every decision for her, unable to decide such simple things as what sandwich she wanted at a restaurant. I became less a husband

and more like a father to a child; she was growing younger and simpler. How could I approach her, how could I make love with Jan when her magnificent sensual womanhood was ebbing away?

I would touch her—by now, it was always me starting this—and she would roll over and put her hand on me. She would stroke my chest, up and down, up and down. And I realized she wasn't making love. She had forgotten what we were doing, what was next, how to touch me. She had forgotten her desire. At first I would guide her hands. But as time went on, I would just let her hand slowly brush my chest until her eyes closed and she drifted into sleep. The Disease had taken this away from us. There was no revenge to exact, no one to blame, no point to anger.

It is surprising what a person will accept. Maybe we say we do it out of love, and that would be sweet and nice to believe. But I accepted this because there was no other choice. And I still had her in my life, as much as she could be. If this one part was gone, the private passion that brings together two people who love each other, then my job was to adjust, and so I did. I think about her now and how we made a thousand nights of memories. We used to joke about how we would chase each other around the old folks' home strapped in our wheelchairs because surely our passion would never end. I think of all the nights that should have been, all the memories we were yet to make.

They, too, are gone.

Walking Into Oblivion: Stage Five

Major gaps in memory and deficits in cognitive function emerge. Some assistance with day-to-day activities becomes essential. At this stage, individuals may be unable during a medical interview to recall such important details as their current address, their telephone number or the name of the college or high school from which they graduated . . . become confused about where they are or about the date, day of the week or season. (Seven Stages of Alzheimer's Disease from www.alz.org, the Alzheimer's Association)

With Jan, the occasional lapses became the everyday lapses. She would read something out loud to me from the morning paper, and minutes later read me exactly the same passage. At first it was annoying, but in time I got used to it. A new normal.

In Asia, we lived a two-country life, moving back and forth between Tokyo and Beijing with ease. We had clothes in both places so, if we planned right, we could travel without a suitcase. Except, of course, we were never that clever, and I was forever reaching for a tie or shirt and realizing . . . oh . . . it's in the other apartment.

Jan used to pack for both of us when we went on trips, her way of helping. She was good at it, but in time that stopped. And then, in time I had to go in and repack her suitcase before the trip because her suitcase would be stuffed with clothes, some for winter and others for summer, no matter the season. There might be heavy cashmere sweaters when we were going from sweltering Tokyo in August to smoggy and broiling Beijing, where it would be even hotter.

So I went through the suitcases and carefully removed what she didn't need. If I did it just before we left for the airport, it worked. If I did it the night before and then went into work for a bit the next morning, she would repack the sweaters while I was away and without my knowledge.

Switching cities began creating a disorientation that left her feeling ever more helpless. We would travel from Tokyo to Beijing, between our two familiar apartments and, as time went on, it would take her two or three days to figure out that we had changed places. And in time, she completely lost track of the country she was in and tried to pay for things in the wrong currency and, finally, tried to pay for everything using dollars.

For a while—and only for a while after the diagnosis—she was aware of her own confusion. She would say repeatedly: "I know I have this . . . thing . . . in my head. Am I okay?"

Yes, darling, I would answer, using my matter-of-fact voice, hoping my calm tone would reassure her.

"I don't want to be a burden," she would repeat over and over. "I can just go away. Why don't I just go away?"

No, darling, I would say. I will take care of you. Wouldn't you take care of me?

"Yes!" And the idea of being a burden would fade . . . for a while.

9

"Walking with a friend in the dark is better than walking alone in the light."
~Helen Keller

How Did They Know, and Thank God

If there is something good here, it came not from within me but from how others helped me. Some were friends already, others were strangers who became friends by reaching out. I didn't realize how solitary caregiving would be, and I underestimated how much I needed help. My excuse was that I was the amateur trying to force aside a field of dense fog by waving my bare hands.

Being overseas had made us exotic and interesting, the well-traveled couple worthy of a dinner invitation. Now what was good about that life played against us. In Asia I was isolated from the most normal kind of help, which was about getting insight from others fighting the same disease. I tried finding a support group in Tokyo, but what groups they had were all in Japanese and only for those with elderly parents or aged spouses suffering from Alzheimer's. Japan's culture discouraged people from talking or sharing much about their personal lives, so there was little help for me there. And Japanese doctors didn't have the kinds of medications available that I could get in the United States.

But a group formed around me from different parts of the world, small but effective. Harry Dank first met Jan in 1986. He's one of those rare people who likes to work overnight, and this has served him well at his job at CBS Radio News. That meant he was on duty at night in New York during our daytime in Asia. He was often the one who called Jan to get a story done when she was the radio stringer on our first posting in Tokyo.

When Jan was diagnosed, Harry became a human search engine, keeping me up to date on stories about new research, drug trials, and the occasional hope from potential breakthroughs. It helped that he spent five days a week, eight hours a night, reading the news wires. He would forward stories on Alzheimer's as they appeared.

But mostly he called with two questions: How's Jan? And equally important: How are you? Being a fellow journalist he expected the truth, and that meant I had to tell him the truth, which meant I had to put those things into words. That question always made me pause and consider where I was in the journey, and explain to him how I was doing at this point or that. It was a kind of talk-about-it therapy, don't hide from those feelings, and that worked.

While I will always be eternally grateful to Harry and how he helped me, I stood in awe of the instinctive abilities of others to understand what Jan needed because there were so many times when I felt both lost and unsure how to respond to her changes. I was forever reading books or checking the latest website on Alzheimer's, but some people were just born to have that insight. One such person was Billie Tisch. Her late husband, Laurence Tisch, was the CEO of the CBS Television Network from 1986 to 1995, and I was lucky and grateful to know them well.

Early on during his ownership, he and Billie visited Tokyo to see the CBS News Bureau and there was a small dinner where Billie met Jan. Billie sent a thank you note and said what a lovely time she had; how much she liked Jan, and that we should keep in touch. And we did. If Billie and Larry were somewhere traveling where we were, like London, we would meet for dinner. If we were in New York, we would try to match schedules for the same.

Petite and incredibly gracious, Billie was also always wise beyond my comprehension. There are rare and good people like that. She sent me a note once. I have it still:
"I hope that as Jan's memories fade, you can dig down for thoughts of easier earlier times together and that your treasured recollections bring smiles of what was, rather than sadness for what is lost."

We visited New York once after Larry died and shortly before I had to move Jan into an assisted living facility. We had dinner with Billie at the home of her son and his wife, Andrew and Ann Tisch. For no special reason, she gave Jan a gift of a small scarf. I believe it was red, one of Jan's favorite colors. I asked her later if she had read up on Alzheimer's and wanted to give Jan a memory cue, and she said no. The idea of giving Jan a present was something she did from instinct. I remember it being a hard night for Jan. There were seven people chatting with each other around the table, something she would have once loved. No more. She went quiet. Through the evening, she uttered two sentences and that was it. But the scarf . . . she remembered that for weeks afterward. Whenever she wore it, she'd say, "Oh, that was from Billie, where we had that lovely dinner."

Did she remember the dinner conversation? Not at all. But she remembered the scarf, and it reminded her of Billie, and that somehow connected to "a" dinner. And that pleased her. And thrilled me.

There was also help from another long-time friend that Jan liked and admired. Amy Bickers had worked in London, Hong Kong, and Tokyo, where she was the Bureau Chief for Voice of America. She and her husband, Chaz, moved to Seattle when they decided it was time to raise their two rambunctious American boys in America with a backyard that could absorb some of their endless energy. Amy has the same upbeat, just-get-it-done personality that Jan once embodied. Amy has a lot of the same restless energy that Jan had, and it was now spent raising two boys, jogging every morning, and still finding time to work a full-time job.

She has always radiated a spirit of caring for those important to her, and with Jan's diagnosis, Amy was almost immediately at hand and ready to help. She and Jan started as colleagues who became friends after they first met in London and worked for CNN. They seemed fated to work together. When we moved back to Tokyo and Jan began free-lancing for VOA, Amy was, by then, living and working in Hong Kong and was one of the VOA editors who took in Jan's stories. VOA moved her to Tokyo where, until they left for America, she and Chaz lived in our apartment building a few floors below us. Being Amy, she was not convinced when, during a phone call from Seattle, I told her I was "all right" after Jan's diagnosis in

2005. Typical of Amy, she went to work finding ways of helping Jan and me.

"You need support," she said. Being a reporter, she reached for the tool she knew best . . . the telephone. Phone call after phone call, one conversation led her to another source or idea. Those collections of information led to an e-mail that left me humbled for the thorough work she had done, and the care she was bringing to Jan's plight and my confusion:

Dear Barry, Here are some resources to get you started.

Some? Amy sent me a detailed list of help lines in the US, complete with phone numbers and contact names, people to whom she had personally spoken. She sent suggestions for books, and even had a line on someone she knew in Tokyo who could spend time with Jan. And the e-mail included this:

A man named Dick has a spouse whose wife also has Early Onset. Lives in the Seattle area.

I called Dick Lundgren immediately. Dick's wife, Dorothee, was much further down the road than Jan with Early Onset Alzheimer's Disease. Her descent was so similar to Jan's that I felt Dick could warn me of the pitfalls ahead. And he was honest enough that I sensed he would share the mistakes he made along his way, so I could avoid making the same ones. In time, I came to describe him as my Alzheimer's Buddy. He was the lighthouse in my fumbling darkness because Dorothee was more advanced. It was as if Jan and Dorothee were in a parallel universe, and Jan's changes mirrored what Dorothee had already passed through. Dick and I as caregivers watched and coped, for better or worse, from the outside.

Dorothee's symptoms first showed in 1995, and she was finally diagnosed in 2001. Dick retired in 2003 to become her full-time caregiver. In January, 2008, she was functioning so poorly that Dick felt he could no longer help and realized he could no longer cope, and he finally placed her in an Adult Family Home. Dick would look back and use his own experiences to ease my confusion. Since he was also active in Alzheimer's support groups, he could also draw on shared conversations with those others going through this with us. He was better than a book or website because he was a friend.

The first question we discussed was whether I should tell people about the diagnosis. There are pretty much only two answers—you share or you hide. Dick said people in his Early Onset support groups did both, and those who were most successful were the ones who were open with friends and family from the beginning. This made sense. People already noticed changes in Jan, and it would only get worse. They needed to know what was going on so they could adjust both their thinking about Jan and how they dealt with her when we got together. That also meant reducing the number of awkward moments for Jan when we were with other people. This, I desperately wanted.

Dick helped me shape guidelines I could share with friends on how to prepare for being around Jan: be patient with the constant repetition of sentences, understand why she will tell you the same story three times in ten minutes or, conversely, why she will sit without talking for an hour or more.

And he helped me with an early crisis that was a warning of how Alzheimer's was playing cruel tricks on Jan's brain by altering what she could remember. As I explained to Dick, it unfolded this way:

I am feeling a bit overwhelmed. I've seen some things in Jan that alarm me, and I'm wondering how they match your experiences.

Example: The Sunday of our Seattle visit, Jan's dad had a conversation with her about his will (I wasn't there). Jan came downstairs in tears, saying her dad was throwing her out of the will because we had enough money. Jan took this as rejection, and that she was being separated from her two brothers and two sisters.

BUT - when I talked with Jan's father, he was dumbfounded. He said he didn't tell her he "cut" anyone out of the will, only told her that he would probably give most of what money he has to the grandchildren for college. To him, it was a casual conversation, not a planned confrontation. This was just Jan and Dad talking about his priorities for his estate.

It was a first look into what would be more and more common; that what I, or others, told Jan was not getting through as we said or meant it. More importantly, she could not give me

an accurate sense of what others were saying to her. Her
memories were being filtered and distorted in unpredictable
ways.

Dick had already been there, as he wrote:

> *I understand exactly what you are talking about. I went
> through this with Dorothee, and still do from time to time.
> She was telling me things that I knew were not so. She
> would get things in her head and, no matter what I said, I
> could not change her mind. I learned that the only way to
> get around this was to first appear to agree with her. Then if
> it was due to something she told me someone had told her,
> I'd contact that person directly to get the correct
> information. I could then decide to address it to Dorothee or
> just let it go. I no longer give anyone my home phone
> number, just my cell.*

He warned me that I would see The Disease making its
changes in sometimes small and subtle ways. He called them
"Little Windows" into Alzheimer's. As I watched our lives
change and felt us withdrawing from the world, Dick sent me
this:

> *Dorothee went through this for a while where she
> didn't really want to go anywhere. In hindsight I think she
> was concerned that she would do something that would be
> embarrassing for her and that people would notice and
> figure out that she had Alzheimer's. The other thing that
> could be happening is that there are a number of different
> steps that Jan has to do to get to the market. For instance,
> leave the apartment, get on the elevator, remember which
> button to push and floor to get off on, leave the building,
> etc. I think you get where I'm going.*
>
> *You and I do this without thinking about it, but a
> person with Alzheimer's has to work at thinking and
> remembering everything to do. This is where all of the
> confusion starts and grows from. Also, by the time she gets
> to the market she is exhausted from all of the work she had
> to do to get there. Then she has to go through all the steps
> to get the items she went there for. At some point Jan will
> get to where she will not go anywhere without you or
> someone else. She also will walk at some distance behind
> you unless you hold her hand and keep her with you. If I*

don't hold Dorothee's hand she will stop and stay in place
until I get her.

One day, there was an incident with Jan. She got up in
the middle of the night headed for the bathroom. She was
confused, unable to communicate what she wanted.
Moreover, she was stooped and shuffling, more of an
unsteady stumble. It was scary, as if this was some
desperately old person who could no longer walk. I led her to
the bathroom and back and let her sleep late that morning.
When she woke up, she had no memory of what had
happened, not even of getting out of bed.

I needed more than information . . . I needed advice, so I
turned to Dick.

Question: I told Jan about the event – which she didn't
remember – and it scared her half to death. So now I am
wondering if honesty really is the best policy here. Do you
have any advice? I am inclined to NOT talk about these
events with her, should or when it happens again. I don't
see that it helps, and I can see how frightening it is for
her to hear about things that she doesn't remember.

To which Dick replied:

I have found that it is best not to tell Dorothee about most
things like this. It only causes her to cry, and it just isn't
worth it. I also decided long ago that this is the only case
where a "little white lie" doesn't hurt. We have discussed
both of these in my support groups and all have come to
the same conclusion.

Then there were the little changes that altered little
routines, and yet became a constant reminder of The Disease.
One was a penchant she developed for collecting and rearranging things for no reason. I first noticed this one
morning when I went to take a pill and the bottle wasn't on
the bathroom shelf where I usually left it.

At first, it was no big deal. I figured I must have moved it
and went about opening drawers and looking on other shelves.
Something prompted me to check the top of the bedroom chest
where we kept Jan's medications and, sure enough, mine was
there as well. At some point in the day she had gone through the

house collecting all the bottles that looked like medications and then carefully arranged them on the chest.

There was no use asking her why, because she wouldn't remember the doing or the reason. But I wondered if this was a new pattern, and one to be often repeated.

To Dick, it was a reminder of little things that add stress on the caregiver, layer by layer, and a sign that I was moving quickly down the same road where every aspect of day to day life is increasingly unpredictable and exhausting because it needs particular thought, preparation, and more patience. His note about Dorothee:

Oh yes . . . the hiding or rearranging of things is very familiar. Dorothee took everything out of her dresser about four years ago and then put it all back but in different drawers. Then she accused me of giving her things away because she couldn't find them. She would also take her doll collection and hide them in different places and forget where they were. She would tell me that someone had stolen them. I finally put them on top of her dresser, which she can't reach.

This all took place when I was still trying to reason with her and that made it more frustrating for me. I learned quickly not to try to reason with her. It doesn't work.

I don't know how you get your personal mail but I would suggest a P.O. Box or some way that she can't access. They have the tendency of hiding incoming and outgoing mail. I know of some people that had real nightmares with this issue. Water, power shut off. Collection agencies, etc.

I am sure you heard me talk about my spending "months" looking for Dorothee's glasses. I found them in the strangest places . . . the pantry, the hutch with all of her collectables from Germany, even on the hanger I have attached to our patio door so she doesn't walk into the door. I finally gave up and she doesn't wear them anymore. Too frustrating and time consuming.

Old friends who have known Jan for many years also helped me see where we were. One was Bob Hartstock, a wonderfully creative architect/designer who helped us on several renovation projects at our house in northern California. He worked side by side with Jan on some of the bigger tearing-down-walls remodeling.

After our visit in the summer of 2007, he sent me a note, a snapshot. It wasn't that I didn't see some of these things, but it was that I wasn't registering them, or didn't want to. Bob's note was both analytical and clear:

> It appears that with simple tasks she was confident to proceed, such as rinsing the dishes and loading the dishwasher. This seemed intuitive and she did not question herself. I also observed that she seemed to zone out when completing this task. She would sing and appear to be in a very happy place, in her mind. But with the task of cooking or multi-tasking, she was lost, confused how to proceed, forgetful with the task in hand, and unable to complete the task.

> I think she recognized the problem, but was unable to solve it. Almost like something that had to be done, but she forgot the skills how to complete the task. Cooking dinner: she knew you must cook the steaks, but was unsure how to cook them. And sometimes she was unable to locate the steaks. Travel: she knows she will be traveling, but not sure where or when. Social functions: as long as you are there and in sight she knows she is fine. Although I think she also felt safe with me and I probably was very protective of her, too.

The changes were more obvious to Bob because our visits were sometimes many months apart. To me the progression was incremental and easy to miss. But when I shared this with Dick, he saw something different and ominous. His take:

> It appears that Jan is starting to regress into her own little world. I note Bob's comments about singing and a very happy place. This goes along with the loss of short term memory. This is how Dorothee started before she found her "friends" in the mirror.

In September, 2007, there was a new incident while we were in Beijing; Jan got confused, dizzy, and couldn't stand. We went to the small medical clinic in our hotel. The doctor was concerned about a stroke, so we took an ambulance to a well-equipped Western-style hospital on the outskirts of town, where the cause was quickly identified.

It was a urinary tract infection, and it hit her especially hard. The good news was that it was an easy thing to cure. Yet

something almost routine turned into one of those windows into
The Disease. Jan had a series of tests to help with the diagnosis.
One of them meant giving a urine sample, something almost all
of us has done at some time. But Alzheimer's makes the routine
into the bizarre, as I wrote to Dick.

> *When we took her to the emergency room on Monday for*
> *what turned out to be the urinary tract infection, they*
> *asked her to give a urine sample. Two days later when I*
> *came home I saw a coffee cup in the bathroom full of*
> *urine — somehow she thought she needed to "give" another*
> *sample. She covered it with a note saying "do not touch"*
> *and that it was for a "special lab" that night. Then she*
> *used soap on the mirror to draw arrows at the cup/sample.*
> *Oddly, after the emergency room run on Monday she could*
> *not remember it by Tuesday. But last night (Friday) she*
> *started talking about some of what she remembered.*

There was another facet I could not anticipate. During the
exam in the emergency room the doctor ordered a CT scan, to
make sure there was no stroke, and it came back just fine.
Except they found that the front part of her brain was
beginning to atrophy.

Dick pulled no punches:

> *Brain atrophy is the shrinking of the brain which is, in*
> *reality, the brain dying. This is what happens to the brain*
> *with Alzheimer's. As the neurons can no longer*
> *communicate, they die.*

It was also around this time that I hired what I called the
"Jan Buddies" when we were in Beijing. They were English-
speaking Chinese women, often young college graduates, who
could be with Jan and give her the confidence to go out and
about in Beijing since she didn't speak the language. Having
someone with her also meant she never felt panicky about the
chance of getting lost. I began seeing a new pattern of Jan —
trying to hide the changes — and she did this with an innate
cleverness by compensating for what she couldn't remember.

As an example, she and her "Jan Buddy" went to a local
frame shop. When I got home that night, I casually asked when
the framing would be done. She couldn't remember, so she came
back with a different answer. "They work pretty fast."

She was increasingly taking notes, writing down the simplest of chores. In the Beijing apartment, we usually called room service for dinner. She started writing down our order because she could not keep in her mind "hamburger" or "pasta" even for the minute or two it would take to walk to the phone and call room service and give the order. It was a sign, as if I needed one, of how her short term memory was so far gone.

I asked Dick if this was all about compensation. He offered a look into the future that was tough to take.

You are extremely correct. Alzheimer's patients in the early stages are very clever in the ways that they compensate. They all do different things. Some like Jan write things down or give a general answer. Dorothee would answer my questions with other questions. She would also act as though she didn't hear me when it was quite clear she did, so I would ask the question again. Unfortunately, this will only last for while, and then Jan won't be able to make the notes or have the ability to answer the simplest of questions. This took Dorothee about two years before she wasn't able to compensate anymore.

It was about this time that I realized how the personal toll on me was building. I was now the living embodiment of the Alzheimer's book title: *The 36-Hour Day*. The days felt like they were very much 36-hours long, or more. I couldn't change the amount of care that Jan needed, and yet I needed a break to get back my own energy.

Dick told me about his going away on a trip, taking a break from being a full-time caregiver and how he found it rejuvenating. I decided to try the same thing, even though I was uneasy about leaving Jan. Yet, this needed to happen. It was the beginning of acknowledging my exhaustion and, while I still didn't see it as clearly as that, I at least understood the need for a change.

The opportunity came because I had a problem with my eye. I had surgery done in San Francisco, and the doctor wanted me back for a follow up exam. I booked the flight but changed my usual habit of calling friends when I was visiting there. I didn't have the energy to face anyone, a sign of my tiredness. And I was also tired of talking about the changes in Jan to other people, dear though they were. Each recitation was a reminder of what was happening to her, and each reminder was about what I was losing. I needed a break from this, as well. It felt selfish but it was a much-needed physical and mental recess. It also meant sleeping for hours in a hotel, maybe watching TV, ordering from room service, and not talking.

It was exactly what I needed. The world went on for two days without me. I slept a lot and walked a little, and allowed myself the intense pleasure of doing nothing. I thought myself wise, because I would come home rested and recharged and better able to care for Jan.

Then The Disease crept in, taking advantage of my absence by taking Jan down a little more. The trip to San Francisco was a turning point, becoming the end game of how I was then caring for Jan. And it unfolded so innocently and amid my best laid plans for my absence.

While I was in San Francisco, I had two women friends from the Beijing office come to the apartment and take Jan out for breakfast at our hotel coffee shop. One came one day, the other the next, and my intent was both so she would have company and make sure she was okay and also to check that she had taken her pills. They were loaded in a day-by-day dispenser that stretched across the week.

How clever of me, right? It set my mind at rest knowing Jan would be monitored. Upon my return, I discovered that my clever plan was a flop. While I was gone she took all the pills out of their compartments, the entire week's doses, and rearranged them. There were too many this day, not enough for the next. The friends couldn't know this, since their job was to inquire whether Jan had taken her pills, and Jan confidently answered both days, "Yes."

Changing the pills was new and dangerous behavior for her. My day job was often about traveling, and now I realized I couldn't leave her alone for even a day because she might re-do her pills again.

And even though I knew better, I was still surprised at how changes could happen so quickly, and how I was caught in this constant struggle to accept, adjust and surrender to another reality-adjustment, another new normal. And there was a new normal I now had to accept.

It was time for Jan and me, who seemed to have everything we needed by just being together and who cherished our alone time, to realize that we could no longer have that. I needed to make another change—a full-time live-in caregiver. I'd reached the point where I could no longer trust her with her own pills.

The next phase of my caregiving job was now about finding the right person who could move in and help me with Jan. And even though I knew what had to be done, another part of my brain ached over yet another ending of Barry and Jan. But if she could no longer be left alone, then I could no longer care for her by myself. Our Barry and Jan private life . . . what nourished and delighted and sustained us . . . was ending. Not changing, not shifting, not adjusting. Ending. And not only would we never get it back, this ending was but a prelude. There were more endings out there, and I needed to face each new one, to incorporate and adjust. More than anything, I needed time. But The Disease was accelerating. It didn't care how fast Jan was changing. It set its own pace. It moved at its own time.

Maybe it sensed victory as it robbed her, and that made it hungrier to claim more of her ever faster—quickly and without mercy. The Disease mocks not just the one whose mind it is stealing, but the others around her trying to fight back.

Only now there was no fighting back. The retreat had begun.

TIMELINE
Fall, 2007
Barry's update to family and friends

Jan had her annual visit to the neurologist where she took what is called the Mini Mental Test. It checks for memory, cognition, thinking processes, etc. The highest score is thirty. Anything below twenty-seven indicates trouble. Last year Jan scored fifteen and this year it dropped to six.

The loss of memories from what we do during the day is incredibly sad for me. I try to plan special things to help her. For instance, in the roughly four weeks we spent on vacation in northern California, we dined with friends every night but one. I wanted Jan socializing to the hilt. Yet when all was said and done, much of it was lost to her. "It's just a blur" she said one night about what we had done that day.

Her once endless taste for travel is drying up because it is hard for her to remember where we are if we are in strange surroundings like a new hotel room.

She remains constantly cheerful and upbeat, which is wonderful and yet, in some way, makes it worse. It is a reminder of what a sweet and optimistic person she is.

We have entered the "I don't know" chapter. I don't know what Jan will be like when she wakes up, or when I come home from the office, or in the evening before or after dinner. The things I am seeing are bewildering and confusing and, for her, frightening with fewer than ever words to express herself.

This is prompted by a change in our reality. We are now joined by a live-in caregiver, Diane Malone, who flew with us to Asia from her home in Tacoma when we returned from the US in mid-October. Diane is amazingly calm, with wisdom that comes from her experience as a nurse in everything from frenzied military medivac C-130 airplanes in the Persian Gulf War to the gentle calm of working in an old people's home.

Having a caregiver meant telling Jan that she can no longer go outside alone – not to the grocery store, or the gym, or for a walk. It triggered a combination of rage and fear as she understands and loathes herself ("I don't want to be a burden") for what is going on.

The rage is something I have never seen in her – a fist clenched, red-faced, physically uncontrollable shaking fury. It was first aimed at Diane who personified the new limits to her freedom, but now she realizes (sometimes) that it is really anger about having Alzheimer's. It comes and goes, this thunderous or deeply sullen rage, often triggered when we tell her that she can go anywhere but now she must always be accompanied. The fear is, in truth, harder for us all. She knows or senses what she is losing – memories and her freedom – "I'm losing my mind, aren't I" – but not how to stop it or fight it.

Diane and I tell her that going out, seeing new things and having new experiences will stimulate her brain, working it like you work a muscle to get it into shape. We call ourselves – Jan, Diane and me – the "Jan Team," working together. Sometimes we widen the team so it includes all of you, the people of her life, often by name. She understands and embraces this . . . sometimes.

When the understanding and the comfort of remembering friends fades, the only thing left is fear. Then all she wants is to cling to me, as if somehow my arms and closeness can protect her. I hold her a lot these days, whenever she needs it. Sometimes, it seems like I am holding a terrified child afraid of lightning flashes, and storms, and things she can't understand.

Her fear is contagious. I feel it looking into her face and knowing that some part of her is no longer there, that she is no longer my Jan except when she is – and then not knowing when it will be gone again. After morning coffee? Before dinner? All day? Not today?

Most of my tears these days come from this: for the first time, I have seen her panic as she feels herself change, as she grasps tightly to memories and experiences, as if holding on means they won't go away, and she begs within herself to somehow get better so she can go back to being the independent optimist she once was.

Part of me wonders if I should share these personal thoughts with you. Please understand that this is incredibly hard for me. But those who have gone through this warn me of the danger of the stress to the caregiver. I've resolved to remain as open as I can allow myself to be, if only because I'll be of no use to Jan if I falter under the pressure of what's going on.

I've written before about losing my best friend as Jan changes. The other day I realized something else that hit me hard. It is not fear – fear has been my midnight companion since this started. It is that given all *the time we spend together, I am increasingly alone. I will hold tight to her hand for the whole journey, but all my tears cannot stop that she is moving ever slowly . . . away.*

We do a lot of explaining reality these days — explaining the new circumstances, why we have a caregiver, why she can no longer go out alone. And I hold her, even though I can no longer protect her against the terror of knowing.

~Barry

10

"Dare to reach out your hand into the darkness, to pull another hand into the light."
~Norman B. Rice

Now We Are Three

On a lovely crisp October day in 2007, United Flight 876 from Seattle glided gently onto the runway at Tokyo's Narita Airport in mid-afternoon. It fulfilled the measure of what I consider a good flight—it was perfectly uneventful.

Jan and I had made this trip many times before. Only this time, it wasn't routine. This time we were not two. We were three because retired nurse Diane Malone came to Asia as our new live-in caregiver. I reached the point where I knew I could no longer leave Jan alone, even when I was at the office, and certainly not if I needed to travel somewhere for days (or weeks) on end. And travel without warning was a normal part of my job.

One big reason for full-time care was Jan's increased disorientation. She would rarely leave the hotel in Beijing, except with the "Jan Buddies" I hired on an occasional basis, so that wasn't a worry. But in Tokyo, she would still get into the cab by herself and tell the driver in Japanese how to take her to the grocery store several neighborhoods over that specialized in serving foreigners. And lately she began buying the same things over and over. We had enough bottled water in the pantry to float a Navy destroyer, but still more would be delivered after each shopping trip. I wondered how soon it would be before she got to the grocery store and forgot how to tell a Japanese cabbie how to get her home. There was no answer. I would only discover after it was too late, after she lost her way or just got lost, period. I couldn't risk it. It was time for outside help.

I advertised on craigslist in Denver, CO, and Portland, OR. Denver because my daughters could handle interviews and Portland because I had always liked the city and felt I could find someone nice in that nice place. Excuse the lack of logic here, but I was floundering.

There was one applicant who was young, about eighteen or twenty, and was a swimsuit model. "Could I take time off if I get a modeling gig?" I decided that when moving another woman into your house to care for your wife, a swimsuit model was probably not going to be a confidence builder for Jan.

There was another applicant who broke up with her boyfriend and thought being in Asia would help in her healing process. Thanks, but no. Others were better, real candidates, and we interviewed and checked references. Then we found Diane, who lived in Tacoma, WA. Again, it was Dick, my Alzheimer's Buddy, to the rescue. He put out the word to people in the local Alzheimer's community that someone in Asia was looking for a live-in caregiver, and it reached Diane from a friend of a friend. If there are miracles, was this not one?

She was amazingly qualified, having worked in long-term care facilities. As a Licensed Practical Nurse, she had done ward duty and understood not just sickness, but the patience that any nurse needs in dealing with the ill and their families. She also had a successful military career, serving thirteen years in the Air Force Reserve, and nine years in the Army National Guard. Her duties consisted of supervising teams doing medical evacuations (medivacs) from places like the Middle East during the first Gulf War, and a volunteer stint in New Orleans with the Red Cross in the aftermath of Hurricane Katrina. I had to wonder why in the world she wanted to work with me for what was little more than slave wages. The answer turned out to be that she was not only between challenges, but she also had a sense of adventure. Living in two Asian cities—Tokyo and Beijing—sounded irresistible to her.

I explained to Jan that Diane was coming to live with us to help out. At first, it went well, starting from that October day when we landed at Narita and headed for our apartment. In Tokyo, Diane slept on a futon in the third bedroom. In Beijing, since we only had a one-bedroom apartment, we found someone who wanted a roommate for an apartment nearby. I paid Diane's half of the rent and this meant that we were settled in both cities. I congratulated myself on getting it right.

From October to Christmas, Jan was in the mode of what Diane called "touring and showing you my city." Jan wanted to share Tokyo and Beijing with Diane, the way any gracious person would treat a houseguest. I have pictures from those days, Jan and Diane wandering through parks and sightseeing. At this early stage, the idea of a live-in caregiver didn't bother Jan, although there was finesse needed on everyone's part. Diane suspected what I didn't; that these early days were a fragile honeymoon. Jan didn't really understand yet that we had a live-in caregiver because she was faltering. We got a break from the season because the fall was warm and pleasant, and Jan loved the excursions with Diane. Jan had always been the first in line for sightseeing or visiting a new museum, so life hit a pleasant stride.

Diane remembered those early days this way:

"When Jan didn't want to venture out I would ask her about the collection of artwork from various parts of the world that filled the apartment. She explained, in great detail, where each piece came from, and always with great joy. I laugh at the memory of her showing me the four-foot tall women carvings from Bali. Now these women aren't that appealing, but Jan had wanted them for the beautiful carving. When I said, "but Jan these women are not all that attractive," she would answer, "Oh, I know, but aren't they a hoot to look at!

"The apartment has several Tibetan chests that you had brought back from your travels from that area. When the afternoon sunlight came through the windows each day these chests would be all aglow with colors of red, green and gold. The detail jumped out at you to say 'look at me, read between the lines of color to read of my history.' Jan loved these chests and she would spend afternoons rearranging their contents.

"The sofa and chairs were draped in fabrics of red, yellow and gold ever so tastefully, giving the room the feeing of elegance, warmth, grace and style."

But then came a new phase, where Jan slipped a little more into a different world populated by people only she knew. Diane

sent this e-mail when I was on assignment, and I think even she
was taken aback.

> *She is going through the flat moving this and that. "Getting*
> *ready to get rid of stuff, to make room for all the people." She*
> *asked me to make arrangements to have most of the furniture*
> *taken out of my room. She took everything out of the big blue*
> *suitcase and is now taking those items from room to room.*
> *When I said to her, "Jan, just you, Barry, and I live here," her*
> *response was, "I know but more people are coming and are*
> *here now." I just let her be, and she soon settled down at the*
> *computer. I ask her to check the news for me, and this helps*
> *most of the time.*

Diane was seeing what I had experienced, that Jan was losing
her sense of where she was that day. If we flew from Beijing back
to Tokyo, it might take Jan three or four days to understand where
she was even though she and Diane were walking the streets of
Tokyo almost daily.

There was the same confusion when we flew to Beijing. Jan
would be in the Beijing one-bedroom apartment with China out
the window, and two or three days after we made the switch she
would still be asking, "What city are we in?"

And there was now restlessness and unease that triggerd her
desire to go somewhere, almost anywhere. And this mood came
with no warning. One day Diane and Jan were at a museum, and
Jan suddenly stood up and announced that she was, indeed, going
"home."

"I have a credit card and money," she said, insisting that
"Barry called," and told her to fly to Seattle. It was a moment for
surgical cleverness, so Diane told Jan there was no problem about
going to the airport, but it was late and all the flights to Seattle
that day were already gone.

"You would have to spend the night in the airport," Diane
said. "I've done that, Jan, and it's really uncomfortable. There's no
place to sleep except on those benches."

Maybe they could just go tomorrow? Diane suggested.

Jan decided that sleeping for hours on uncomfortable
airport plastic seats wasn't a good idea and sat back down. In a
minute she had forgotten the whole idea. But when Diane told
me, I knew this was another step further away. "It was her

stubbornness and confusion about time and place," Diane told me later. "It's an example of how quickly Alzheimer's Disease can affect a mind."

When Jan's mood would abruptly change, Diane reacted just as quickly, like when they were on the Tokyo subway. Jan became agitated, anxious to get off "right now" at whatever was the next stop. She was tapping her fingers, and her mood was dark and angry.

Again, Diane reacted quickly and tried to distract her by suggesting they sing a song from a movie Jan and I had watched the night before. This was not normal Tokyo subway behavior, Diane recalled. In Tokyo, everyone keeps carefully to themselves, and it is impolite to even make eye contact with someone else, let alone make noise.

"There we were, two grown women, singing while swaying back and forth among the ever so rigid Japanese."

Diane soon learned the value of the "singing" distraction and used it often in our neighborhood when they were out for walks. "Many times we walked down the street singing, which was a familiar habit for us. We walked as though no one was listening or looking, and we sang as though we were the hit of the show."

I marveled at the thought of them strolling and singing down Tokyo's winding streets, and the Japanese almost too polite to stare at the strange foreign women. I knew Jan was happy if she was singing. I gave myself a nice mental pat on the back because having Diane there was working well for Jan. They got out of the apartment and went sightseeing, which I hoped was stimulating her brain. And it was making Jan feel good at the same time.

When we were together at night, there were conversations about where they had been that day, what they had seen, and a chance to see the pictures they had taken of each other. This was a new normal I could embrace, one that was giving Jan pleasure.

I loved it, and I could feel my anxieties about Jan's care begin to ease.

And then came absolute disaster: The Anger Monster.

TIMELINE
December, 2007
Barry's update to family and friends: Preparing friends for our Christmas visit

Recently we started dealing with a new emotion; defiance. Jan simply refused to go out of the Tokyo apartment because it was "too cold." I finally got her moving by taking the three of us to lunch, but it was an unpleasant new wrinkle. This is the first time she has ever defied ME in a situation like this, since she usually considers me her safe harbor.

Jan has devised several ways to deal with her forgetfulness. The first is ANGER – "I don't care about that person, so why should I remember him/her?" The second is PRETENDING; just agreeing when I really suspect she can't remember. The third, and I see this when we socialize, is going SILENT. I think she is afraid of saying something that draws attention to her situation, so she opts to say nothing at all. I have devised some counter strategies.

When she is angry, I explain who the forgotten person is and why that person is important to her. Humor helps here, and the idea is to jog her memory. Remember that the anger is really directed at herself over what it happening to her, not at any of us. When she's pretending, I just keep right on with the conversation and try to casually drop the name in within the next sentence or so.

Jan might say: ". . . that woman you work with."

Barry: "Yes, you're right, darling, I think Marsha wants to do that story."

And we're off and running.

With silence, the first thing is to notice it and then gently draw her into the conversation. She does fine once she gets comfortable. She is more likely to go silent in small groups, like a dinner, than at larger gatherings. She said virtually nothing – and I mean like two words – at a dinner with a group of eight. Two days later, at a wedding with a group of eighty, she was a social butterfly chatting to one and all and had a great time.

To be honest, she is not going to remember some of you. She is still there, that bubbly charming lady that we all know, so keep that thought if her mood suddenly shifts.
~Best, Barry

11

"Not to have control over the senses is like sailing in a
rudderless ship, bound to break to pieces on coming in contact
with the very first rock."
~Mahatma Gandhi

Comes the Anger Monster

It would erupt usually in the early afternoon, often with only the quick warning of a shadow crossing Jan's face, and then she was in a fury. Sometimes she couldn't even tell us what she was angry about, but the anger was there. Fist clenched. Face red. Sputtering.

It began after Christmas and a visit back to the US that went well and fueled my hopes that we were settling down—that The Disease had backed off for a while. I sent an e-mail out on how to act with Jan and our friends and family responded well.

On Christmas we were in Denver, visiting the girls. My son-in-law's parents are divorced, so we spent Christmas Eve with his mother and her husband, and Christmas Day with his father, Tom and Mary, his stepmother. Adding to the spirit of the season was our new granddaughter.

At Tom and Mary's house the gathering was fairly large, about a dozen people. When Tom saw Jan he introduced himself, as I had suggested in the e-mail. Mary did the same, and Jan was comfortable as she settled into the dinner and chatted with Mary, girl to girl. It felt like a Christmas should feel . . . good food, generations of family, and granddaughter Ariel reminding one and all of new beginnings and the many joys to come as she grew up.

Then it was back to Japan and big trouble that started the moment we walked in the door of the Tokyo apartment. Diane was there. She had stayed in Japan to sightsee. Over our two week absence, Jan had completely forgotten about Diane and having a caregiver. My constant reminders to Jan about Diane on the flight home were useless.

I don't know (who does?) what triggered the next phase; the anger. It was horrible to see this bright, laughing woman turn on herself and everyone else with such fury, an anger I had never seen before. And she had a target for what bordered on hatred: Diane. In these moments, Jan would insist that she didn't need Diane, and that Diane was in the way. To Jan, having another woman in the house was some kind of proof that she had a disease, and Jan rejected this.

No longer the woman who had once vowed to her neurosurgeon that she would fight and beat Alzheimer's, she was now a woman who outright denied that there was anything wrong with her. Diane was the face-to-face contradiction to that.

"We were never going to win," Diane told me later.

There were days that fooled us, when Jan would be upbeat and friendly.

"Then wham!" remembers Diane. "Out came the anger. Because she had no control, understanding, or coping abilities to handle her anger it was just going to keep coming, making her all the more confused, and agitated.

"I knew, even if she could not articulate it, that Jan suffered with each of these episodes. It was like some kind of uncontrollable fit that would leave her exhausted."

Then it turned out that, in Jan's now fast changing mind, there were others out to get her.

We found this out one day, when Jan was in the midst of her agitation. She was furious about what she claimed were now, not just Diane but, out of nowhere, a total of four women living in the house who frightened her, as if they meant to harm her, along with eating all our food. "Dammit, we have nothing for dinner," she exploded. "It's that Diane and those women. They are eating everything."

Once Jan decided the women were there, they stayed for good. She couldn't describe them, and when I asked something simple like what they were wearing, she said, "Normal clothes, like us."

But over and over Jan said these women were targeting our supply of food, and their leader was Diane. Jan went so far as to confront Diane with the "evidence."

"Jan had taken to hiding her favorite snacks behind tall items only to find them and ask me why I had done that," Diane remembers. "Many times she told me I ate too much and too often, and that I would have to move out by the weekend."

We had given Diane her own small pull-out drawer in the refrigerator where she could store her favorite foods, hoping that would pacify Jan. It didn't. Sometimes Jan would walk me to the refrigerator, her face mottled and red, open the door, and show me how little food there was. "See?" she would say, her finger shaking with rage as she pointed at mostly empty shelves. They were empty because we hadn't bought food for a while.

"Well, darling," I would say, "we can just walk down to the little store and buy some more food."

Buying more food didn't change Jan's moods. The next day, the Anger Monster would come calling. Once she stormed across the little street between our Tokyo apartment building and into the skyscraper where my office was located. I wasn't there, but our sound man was. She told him she had no money to buy food and furiously demanded that he give her cash now! He was taken aback, but he dug into his pocket and handed her Japanese yen. And, of course, she forgot what she had done. It was left to the embarrassed sound man to explain to me that Jan had, well, "borrowed" some money from him.

But it was Diane who was now her main enemy. Jan insisted over and over that if Diane wasn't there our lives would magically get back to normal. We needed to "get rid of THAT woman."

Diane remembers one shopping trip Jan wanted to make without her. "She didn't want me with her. She became hostile, rude, and argumentative. After dealing with this behavior most of the morning my patience had worn thin. I started treating her like a self-centered teenager, with my hands on my hips, looking her in the eye, voice raised just a bit. This helped me more than it did her because I got it off my chest, as they say."

I missed much of the Anger Monster because these outbursts usually came in the early afternoon when I was still at work. By the time I got home, it was late afternoon and Jan shifted into a different and happier mood, making dinner for Barry time. The shift was so fast it was as if someone flipped a switch. Jan would go right to the kitchen to start preparing for dinner. It might only be 3:00 and dinner was at 6:30. But the anger was gone, and now it was the dinner hour and time for all of us to be pleasant.

Even here, The Disease took what it wanted, giving us a more relaxing time with Jan and a much easier time for her without the anger, but it happened with yet another sign that her abilities were relentlessly failing.

"The refrigerator door would open and close, open and close as food was moved around taken out and put back in, moved from one shelf to another," Diane remembers. "The pantry doors were opened and closed many times. She would stand in front of the shelves moving cans and boxes claiming once again 'all the people had eaten the food.'"

The onions and garlic would be chopped with great care, one slice at a time then sautéed until over-cooked.

"It was the chopping process both in the morning and evening that she became obsessed with," Diane recalled, "as this was the one thing she could do without losing her place in the process."

Diane and I both noticed the same things; the meals were getting simpler as multi-tasking in the kitchen became too great a challenge. One evening, after several hours of preparation, we each had one small hamburger patty with a small dollop of ketchup on top.

But I didn't care. She was cooking (with Diane making casual walks through the kitchen through the whole process) and she was happy in her role of taking care of me. These were good things, and I enjoyed them, because by now I knew that whatever Jan was today could and most likely would be different tomorrow.

There was one firm rule—Jan was not to leave the house without Diane. I explained it over and over to Jan, telling her it was my decision and my rule. When she was calm she accepted it peacefully. But when the Anger Monster reared up, all bets were off. And—no surprise—came the challenge that Diane and I both knew was inevitable; abject defiance. One afternoon when I was at work, Jan made it clear to Diane that she was mad and had had enough. She WAS going out shopping on her OWN and

NO ONE was going to stop her. She headed for the front door with escape on her mind. Diane put herself at the front door, using her body to block Jan.

"The afternoon I had to physically stop her was the most challenging," Diane said later. "I had to take her hands, hold tight, look her in the eye and say 'no you cannot leave now.' "

Diane repeated this, over and over, all the while staring directly into Jan's eyes and, at the same time, holding Jan's hands. "I remember taking deep breaths, doing all I could to remain calm and patient."

I realized that the tide was turning. In Jan's eyes, Diane was now human proof that she was somehow ill. As she increasingly rejected Diane, Jan would spend whole afternoons in our bedroom, unwilling to go out of either the Tokyo or Beijing apartment on excursions with Diane. She would stretch out on the bed for hours, awake and uncooperative, with the door shut.

It added a new role to my list of duties, that of peacemaker. I tried reasoning with Jan and telling her why we needed Diane and how her being with us was to help both of us. I watched this rejection of Diane unfold with growing despair. I couldn't battle The Disease alone. I needed Diane or someone else in that role helping me care for Jan. We were way beyond the days when all I needed was to make a phone call or two to make sure she was okay.

But anyone in that role, any extra person in our lives, would become, in Jan's eyes, the same as Diane — proof that something was wrong and that something was about Jan. Occasionally, Jan's anger was directed at me. There would be angry demands that we get rid of Diane, and my efforts to calm her down rarely worked.

There was also anger about money, which was made worse as Jan became more and more befuddled about what country we were in and what currency to use. One trick was to take all the dollars, yen, and Chinese yuan out of her purse and put back only the currency she needed.

That was not the end of it.

"Why don't I have money," Jan would demand, staring angrily at me in the morning as I was on the way to work. "I'm the wife and I should have the money to pay for the groceries."

I would ask her gently, "Did you check your purse?" Usually there would be plenty of money in her purse. She simply forgot to look. Other times I would give her money, and the next day the money would be gone even though she hadn't gone shopping. I never knew where it went, and Diane guessed it got stuck in pockets or under mattresses and that it would turn up some day.

I was so focused on Jan that I missed how this was affecting Diane, who was always upbeat and cheerful in front of Jan and me. But privately she was struggling. No matter how much she counted to ten or went to her room to give her and Jan some separation in hopes of diffusing the anger, she faced what was, at times, an almost unreasoned hatred.

Being ever practical, Diane had a sensible answer to Jan's ill moods . . . exercise. "My morning walks were most important," she says. "It was my way of dealing with anger and stress, and keeping fit mentally and physically. All of which are important when dealing with Alzheimer's. Several times I stepped out onto the dining room balcony, took a deep breath, counted to ten, stretched. Many times Jan would come join me. Sometimes, just being on the balcony and in a different location would help change Jan's own attitude. This gave us the opportunity to diffuse the anger. Soon we would be talking about the view, the little girls on the playground at the school below, or looking at Mt. Fuji."

I had believed that having a caregiver living with us would push the effects of The Disease back for a while because Jan and I could continue some adjusted form of normalcy, even if normal was now a constantly shifting target that I was not always great at hitting.

And at first, Diane agreed, thinking I had bought a few more years living with Jan. With a caregiver, there was consistency and the safety Jan needed. But Diane watched with alarm as the slippage accelerated, and she watched with her own heart breaking. "I would see her clench her fists as she fought so hard to stay involved with a conversation, fighting inside herself not to fade away, trying so hard to stay with us. And then losing it."

Caught in the midst of these changes, and in the losing battle for Jan to accept a caregiver, I forgot that The Disease was wickedly cunning. It hungers for not just the person and the brain it is murdering cell by cell, but also those nearby who are acting out of love and care. If it can pervert that care and love by turning it into destruction, then it can claim two people and it will raise a toast to itself for its deadly clever prowess.

And I knew I was the prime target.

TIMELINE
Spring, 2008
Barry's update to family and friends

There are changes I know are coming and I dread; and one has now arrived. Jan is losing her long-term memory. One of Jan's favorite stories is about birthdays . . . her Dad, her brother Doug and I were all born on January 14th. She was amazed when we discovered this early in our courtship, and it remains her touchstone for why we were fated to be together. The other night at dinner she remembered that there is a "birthday" story and asked me to tell it because she could no longer summon up the details.

I am not sure about sharing these thoughts. I was taught as a good Danish Lutheran child that we just push on and not draw attention to ourselves. But some of you have suggested that knowing what is happening helps understand a disease that we are seeing around us more and more. So I bare something of me, and apologies if it seems too personal. I am not sure how else to share this. Through these past few years, I have lived by one mandate; Jan is paramount in all our thoughts and cares. She is the one with Alzheimer's.

My focus remains getting her good care and the help to battle this — such as having people like Diane, our live-in caregiver, who gets her out of the house and exploring new things. But this disease does not limit itself to one person. Quite the opposite — it takes from all around, especially from those of us too blind to see what it is doing to us. In this case it was my daughter, Julie, who saw and put it succinctly when I saw her over Christmas. She leaned across the table at lunch and told me I was "weary in my soul." And she is right.

Part of it is the simple mechanics of running our daily life — I monitor and pay all the bills, make all the travel arrangements, gently make sure Jan has packed appropriate clothes for a trip, and help her choose from a restaurant menu when she gets lost somewhere in confusion and indecision. But my weariness comes, I think, from a darkness that I discovered is stalking me — loneliness. I have lots of friends. But I no longer have Jan. It sounds like a bad line from a movie. If only. I still remember the moment I knew that I wanted to be with

Jan for the rest of my life. I was driving in a car after visiting her tiny little lakeside apartment in Seattle one evening when it hit me. In my memory, it felt like an earthquake, like something actually shook the car, and in fact, I had to pull the car over. I knew then – with total clarity and for certain – that I needed her in my life, that any sacrifice was nothing compared to being with her, so full of life. (And so darn cute!)

I hear people say that marriage is "hard," that you have to "work" at marriage. I never felt, not one day, that I had to work at our togetherness. We were just . . . us. Sometimes it's easy for me to ignore what is changing because Jan looks so good. But I have realized that she is now someone I need to watch over, like I'm dealing with a child.

I am sorry if I sound somewhat clinical about this. I sometimes think the only way to get through this is by deadening my own feelings because they scare me. They have the potential to overpower and overwhelm me. I could spend every day in tears because there are plenty of moments of private agony and depression. But if I ever falter in front of her, Jan will feel even more frightened. While there are predictable changes, there is no known timeline.

Let's be clear here; Jan still bears the real burden of this disease. She must find ways to cope with the fear and confusion that she tries so hard to hide from all of you. And my focus continues to be on helping her, however I can. But Julie is right. My soul is weary, because I must accept that what I had is slipping away, and when she is gone, my loneliness will be forever.

~Best, Barry

12

"ANXIETY about facing another day and what the future holds.
DEPRESSION begins to affect the ability to cope.
SLEEPLESSNESS caused by a never-ending list of concerns.
EXHAUSTION makes it impossible to complete necessary daily
tasks."
~From Ten Signs of Caregiver Stress by the Alzheimer's
Association

Going Down

People sent me articles warning of caregiver stress and
burnout. This one was especially popular among Alzheimer's
caregivers:

CHRONIC STRESS CAN STEAL YEARS
FROM CAREGIVERS' LIFETIMES
Ohio State University, Sept 18, 2007

COLUMBUS , Ohio - The chronic stress that spouses
and children develop while caring for Alzheimer's
disease patients may shorten the caregivers' lives by as
much as four to eight years, a new study suggests.

The research also provides concrete evidence that the
effects of chronic stress can be seen both at the genetic
and molecular level in chronic caregivers' bodies.

The caregivers also differed dramatically with the
control group on psychological surveys intended to
measure depression, a clear cause of stress.

"Those symptoms of depression in caregivers were
twice as severe as those apparent among the control
group," said Jan Kiecolt-Glaser, a professor of
psychology and psychiatry.

Kiecolt-Glaser said that there is ample epidemiological data showing that stressed caregivers die sooner than people not in that role.

"Now we have a good biological reason for why this is the case," she said. "We now have a mechanistic progression that shows why, in fact, stress is bad for you, how it gets into the body and how it gets translated into a bad biological outcome."

My friends saw what was happening to me from the outside. I did not see it from the inside until Jan faded again, and my deepening level of exhaustion could not be ignored. It began with a behavior I had seen once before in Jan, only now it started showing up more and more frequently.

Sometimes, and always unpredictably, when she would get up at night to go to the bathroom she would be hunched over and muttering nonsense to herself. Her head was drooped down, her eyes downcast and unseeing, and she would shuffle like an infirm, elderly woman. Most dangerous for her was that she had no sense of balance or the automatic reflexes to protect herself. If she fell, she wouldn't react and put a hand out to break her fall or keep herself from hitting something. There was no instinctive sense of self protection and no awareness of any danger from falling.

I would jump up and get in front of her, holding her hands in mine as I walked her to the bathroom. When she was finished, I would guide her slowly back to the bedroom and help her carefully roll into bed. Even this, she could not do alone. And then I would try to go back to sleep.

The frequency was increasing, and the unpredictability meant that every time Jan got up at night, two or three times on average, I woke up on instant red alert. "Where are you going?" If she could answer coherently — "To the bathroom" — I knew it was okay, and I would roll over, wait until she was back in bed and close my eyes and hope for sleep. But if it was the nonsense muttering and the shuffling, I had to jump up quickly to help and protect her.

With this new behavior, which had me up several times a night, it meant that between work and home, I was now working a 24/7 shift. On top of that, I needed to be Mr. Cheerful when I walked through the front door to make sure I kept Jan perked up.

My bad work days had to stay at the office because I could not come home in an unhappy state. That might send her downward as well. My job was to always be upbeat and joking and hope that rubbed off on her. "Honey, I'm home," I would shout, mimicking those 1950s sitcoms. And I would jokingly ask for my 1950s martini, just to round out the act. Jan would always laugh.

I would be chatty at dinner, carrying on more of the conversation as Jan lost her ability to make coherent sentences. Diane and I would talk and when Jan jumped in, we would listen carefully and agree. Even if her sentences made no sense. After dinner, it was on to Jan and Barry time—watching a movie and eating popcorn.

I ended up deciding each night what to watch, usually something from our collection of old black and white movies like *The Thin Man* so we could pretend that Jan and Barry were suave and witty like Nick and Nora.

It was a treadmill, always moving, always demanding. And then there was the growing emotional searing that came from seeing Jan leaving me in front of my eyes. There were times when I decided the only way through this was by deadening my feelings because they scared me. My emotions had the potential to overpower and overwhelm me. And this new night and day, and back into night life was draining my reservoir of energy that I needed to face any new wrinkle.

I could have spent every day in tears, for what point was there in going on? In my mind, going on was about Jan going down. But I couldn't falter, and I couldn't let Jan ever see my tears because it would frighten her. She was beyond understanding difficult emotions, but she would get the message that tears were about my sadness, and this was a message I vowed not to send.

It was Diane who came to my rescue. She suggested that I go out alone once a week for dinner with friends, and she would stay home with Jan and they could watch a movie. Great idea. Except by now, I had no more friends. We had stopped going out long ago. Most of the people we used to see had long since moved away, and the effort of starting over with new people seemed too complicated. I didn't have the spirit and certainly not the energy.

Her second suggestion turned out to be a godsend: Once a month, on her orders, I took a two-night weekend break at a nearby hotel. On Friday afternoon I checked in, usually as soon as the room was available. These were my two days of not waking up because Jan had stirred and not having to constantly put on my happy face. It was not exactly an exciting time by most standards but, in my exhaustion, it was a blessing. I would sleep for ten or twelve hours at night and often nap during the day, and then come home Sunday afternoon.

Diane sold the idea to me by warning that caregivers can collapse. "Before you can help Jan," she counseled, "you must take care of Barry."

Diane had the experience to see what I could not, that Jan was like many Alzheimer's patients in wanting her spouse, the man she was used to having close to her, around especially at night.

Jan was her focus, but she began to get worried about me. "The overeating, drinking, lack of exercise and lack of socialization are taking a toll," she told me. If I did not get rest, Diane warned, I would do what so many other caregivers do . . . forget to care for myself while giving my all caring for the person I loved. And there would be consequences for me.

At first there was resistance to taking the weekend off. My excuses were lame; I was "doing ok," or "the weekends were laid back enough," or "what would Jan say if I'm gone again?" It took just one weekend, and this was a done deal. After that, by Friday of "my weekend," I was at the hotel at 3:01 p.m. to check in the moment they would allow me.

Something odd happened one weekend. Sunday rolled around. The room was typical for a Japanese business hotel, so small that I had to duck getting out of the elevator and out of the shower in the room. The space was cramped, but I didn't care. It was quiet and it was mine, and I had no caregiving duties to perform.

But that weekend, when checkout time rolled around, I did something I had never done before; I didn't go back home. I went to the office. I wrote a script that I had started on Friday and could easily have finished Monday. Then I cleaned out a desk drawer that had been messy for several years.

And then I asked myself — why the hell was I sitting in the office doing stupid chores on a Sunday? Myself answered — because I was not anxious to go back home. Maybe that was proof of how badly I needed some time off. But more upsetting was the sense that I didn't want to re-enter the world of Jan, and The Disease, and the Anger Monster.

I felt no guilt about being away from the apartment for a few more hours because I knew Diane would take excellent care of Jan. I felt guilt about *not* wanting to go back. There was shock about feeling this, a sense that I was finding it harder to be around Jan. She was the woman I cherished through good times and bad. Now I was finding that the frustration of always losing to The Disease might be my defeat.

I vowed to keep going, just keep going. And then my resolve began unraveling. It happened one Sunday afternoon, when I came back from a weekend off. Diane remembered having an alarming thought. "I almost turned you around and sent you back to the hotel for another night," she told me later. She told me I looked tired and anything but rested from a weekend off which was all about getting rest.

That was Sunday. On that Monday I could not get out of bed. I was too tired, and I had never felt like that before. My body felt like a dead weight. I called the office from the bedside phone, said I was ill and immediately fell back to sleep. Through that day I napped fitfully for about eight hours. I was concerned that I wouldn't sleep that night. I needn't have been. I went to bed early and slept a further ten hours.

It was just one more sign that I was in trouble. My weight was up because food was some kind of emotional salve. Living with Diane, a nurse, meant regular checks of my blood pressure, and it was climbing alarmingly, always up a little more than the previous check. I was drinking too much as well. It was a way of self-medicating, and I knew it. I tried to care, but I couldn't. It was like the food was something necessary to get me through today. I'd worry about what it was doing to me tomorrow. Tomorrow, of course, became just another today to get through.

My bosses in New York couldn't help but notice the weight gain, exhaustion, tiredness, and rage, and that was putting me in trouble at the home office. I was in a business that did not favor overweight, aging men who were difficult for crews and producers to work with.

Because I was distracted and exhausted, the scripts I pounded out lacked enthusiasm. Writing is the most sacred part of the job to me—the achingly, thoughtfully sought-for words that communicate what I saw to the person watching—and I was faltering even in this, the part of my craft I had worked all my life to perfect.

And there was the never-ending loneliness. The intimacy was long gone. Jan was no longer a lover, she was now someone that I needed to constantly watch over and care for.

In the midst of this, I had a flashback while working on a routine story. It was a classic symptom of Post Traumatic Stress Disorder. In this instance, an innocuous event triggered memories from covering the Asian tsunami when we were off the coast of Thailand. The tsunami hit on December 26, 2004, and I was in Beijing with Jan and the girls. I had managed to get them all together at Christmas. But then the phone rang, and I was soon on a plane.

It was one of the hardest stories I had ever covered. The death toll was highest among children because they were least able to run, or even realize what was happening. Many were out playing on the beach.

We were in Phuket, Thailand, traveling up and down the surrounding areas that were hardest hit. It wasn't long before we were surrounded by desperate parents and grandparents holding up pictures of children, hoping that somehow their missing kids were in a hospital or had been airlifted out or were in the makeshift refugee camps. But, of course, most were not. Miracles were in short supply.

Buddhist temples became makeshift morgues. Bodies were laid out on the grounds in hopes that family or friends might identify the corpses. I remember seeing many of the dead with their hands raised, as if they were trying to fend off the waters and what would be, for most, a terrifying and certain death by drowning.

One day, as part of our coverage, we were in a boat headed for a story on reef damage from the tsunami. We thought it would be a chance to get away from all the death we had seen. Then, without warning, the boat was suddenly plowing through a field of bleached and bloated bodies that had been washed out to sea when the tsunami hit days earlier.

Now, a year or two later, those horrific scenes flooded back to me in terrifying flashes and sent me racing to a therapist. The PTSD treatment was so intense, quick, and effective, that I failed to take the extra time needed to face up to my ongoing battle with depression, that horror that Winston Churchill called his "Black Dog."

I was on emotional overload and physically exhausted. I was depressed—God knows I can recognize the symptoms—but I just pushed it away. It was all too complicated to worry about just then. Just get me through the immediate PTSD therapy, and life will be better. I didn't have enough emotional reserve to worry about something far bigger and much deeper. And I didn't want to lose my focus on Jan.

I knew ignoring the depression was unwise. Or a better word might be stupid. I could see what was happening to me, where I was headed, and I knew it wasn't good. In truth, I coped by not thinking about the future. Every day was a victory if I just kept moving my feet, kept coming home and cheerfully yelling "Honey, I'm home!" and making Jan laugh with the martini joke.

But the stress of caregiving is well documented, and the long-term effects range from dangerous to fatal. I was now in a legion of stressed out people where one in ten caregivers say their own health is worse because of what they must do, or force themselves to do. Consider just these two sobering research notes from studies quoted by the Family Caregiver Association (www.caregiver.org)

- Higher levels of clinical depression are attributed to people caring for individuals with dementia (such as Alzheimer's). Studies show that 30% to 40% of dementia caregivers suffer from depression and emotional stress.

- In 2005, three-fifths of caregivers reported fair or poor health status, one or more chronic conditions, or a disability, compared with one-third of non-caregivers. Caregivers also reported chronic conditions including heart attack/heart disease, cancer, diabetes and arthritis at nearly twice the rate of non-caregivers (45% vs. 24%).

And with all that, I was better off than most because of my age: stressed-out caregivers aged 66-96 have a 63% higher mortality rate than non-caregivers of the same age. To put it bluntly, caregiving for a loved one is a job that will literally kill you.

Some people sensed what was unfolding and sent me notes and encouragement. One came from the always wise Billie Tisch who told me:

"Just when I think 'older begets wiser,' I am shaken by the realization that, however smart we are, whatever fancy coping mechanisms we have, however deep the love and caring of family and friends from whence our strength cometh, there are situations of profound loss from unfathomable tragedies for which there seem to be no solace or solutions. The weariness you describe, the loss you feel is clearly in that category.

"What I do know, from the 'older' (as above), is that life goes on, and that we don't get to choose regarding the losses which happen to both the loser and the losee. But we do get to choose (if we're lucky) how we handle the aftermath (or in your case, the during-math) of the grief.

"I guess the bottom line of this little dissertation is that one must keep searching for ways to continue to function for one's own well-being and for the salvation, however flawed, of the lost souls, and, importantly, must resist abandoning the hope that one might smile again and find glimmers of light for tomorrow in the darkness of today. Vaya con Dios on this journey.

Love continues to help, and I send mine. Billie"

Diane also tried to warn me, in her own way, but I couldn't hear it from her for a long time, either. She remembers what she thought in those moments. "Barry was hanging from a cliff with one hand and starting to slip with no safety net below."

Diane saw red flares and heard fire alarms going off. She finally sat me down in the living room for a chat. She was careful with her words. "Jan has a disease and, because of that, there will always be people looking after her. But you are the caregiver, and no one is looking out for you."

I thought, who the hell needs to look after me? This is about Jan.

"And you are going down." And she put it bluntly so even I would get it: "You cannot help Jan if you are not here."

I would have given anything to make Jan well, even if my exhaustion, depression, and sleeplessness ended with me not making it. In fact, the reality was just the opposite. All the comfort and care that I was giving, and what it was demanding from me, was not making any difference for Jan.

Ask something of me, anything that will make a difference. But there was no answer.

Walking Into Oblivion: Stage Six

Memory difficulties . . . worsen, significant personality changes may emerge and affected individuals need extensive help with customary daily activities. At this stage, individuals may lose most awareness of recent experiences and events as well as of their surroundings . . . occasionally forget the name of their spouse or primary caregiver but generally can distinguish familiar from unfamiliar faces . . . need help getting dressed properly; without supervision, may make such errors as putting pajamas over daytime clothes or shoes on wrong feet . . . have increasing episodes of urinary or fecal incontinence . . . experience significant personality changes and behavioral symptoms, including suspiciousness and delusions (for example, believing that their caregiver is an impostor); hallucinations (seeing or hearing things that are not really there); or compulsive, repetitive behaviors such as hand-wringing or tissue shredding. (Seven Stages of Alzheimer's Disease from www.alz.org, the Alzheimer's Association)

I remember the first time she forgot me. It was in Beijing. Her current medicines faltered and failed, and we were ramping up to a new one. It has the tendency to upset the digestive system so the dose started small, and during that initiation period she slipped rapidly.

We were in bed, together, and I was stroking her back. She lifted up, looked at my left hand, and said, "You have a wedding ring. Are you married?"

Yes, darling, I am married to you.

In a few minutes it seemed to pass, or did it? By now she was so good at compensating that I couldn't tell if she really remembered me or was just pretending. It was a glance into what was coming. I had read the books, talked with doctors and fellow travelers on this journey.

It was around this time that I met Joan Wieringa, a
registered nurse who spent years in Seattle working in long term
care. She did not know Jan, but she knew a lot about denial. She
shared the story of her husband, ill, failing, and back in the
hospital. It was, in many ways, the story I was now living.

> For the last eight months, many declining physical and
> mental changes had occurred for Dick. I adjusted and just
> believed that when he went into the hospital this time I was
> now experiencing yet one more change and I would adjust
> and cope.

> Late one afternoon a compassionate counselor asked for
> private time with me and kindly but directly told me that
> Dick was near death. At first, I gave her reasons and
> explanations that would allow me to continue the process of
> denial. I finally ran out of words, broke down into tears
> saying NO, NO, NO – only then finally accepting the
> situation for what it was.

> With this acceptance, I could bring our children
> together and tell them that we were near the end of their
> dad's life. We made a plan for a family member to be present
> at all times. Dick died two days later with family present.

Joan had lived denial to practically the last moment of her
husband's life, so she was well-experienced the day she looked
across a table at me, and said bluntly what I didn't want to hear:
"Alzheimer's is a terminal disease. Jan has a terminal disease."

These were words I had run from for years, words I would
not allow myself to either say or think. But denying does not
stop The Disease. It has the endgame already plotted.

13

"On vacations: We hit the sunny beaches where we occupy ourselves keeping the sun off our skin, the saltwater off our bodies, and the sand out of our belongings."
~*Erma Bombeck*

Maui Sun, Sea, Surf and Losing It

It started as a good idea that seemed to just get better. Go on vacation. Get Jan away from her stress about having Diane in the house, get me away from the stress of working by day and caring for Jan at night. Instead, we'd trade the rainy gloom of Tokyo in winter for Hawaiian sun! Sleep late. Sit on a beach. Go to dinner. Let the slow sunsets and easy trade winds of Maui calm and soothe.

I love how drivers on Maui will often pull over to the side of the road that runs along the ocean and get out of their cars, lean against a fender, and just watch the sunset. It's like hitting the pause button on life. And aren't vacations really a pause button, an escape, a chance to shed our daily work clothes and step out of real life?

We had been going to Maui for some years as the girls got older. It was an easy half-way trip; we flew in from Asia, they from the mainland. Everyone spent about the same time on an airplane and there were beaches and snorkeling calling to us all. We always stayed in the same general area around Kapalua and Kahana. It meant that one nearby video rental place still had us in its computer and we knew where the coffee and eggs were in the local grocery store.

What a perfect place to take Jan for a break because here she might remember familiar places, and the sun and bright skies would cheer her up. And maybe cheer me up? The Alzheimer's came along with us, of course, but now I was used to that. The third day we were there, standing in a rental condo and looking west across the water, Jan gazed out the window and said, "Where *are* we?"

"Can't you tell," I asked. "Look out the window."

"It looks nice," she said.

"We're on Maui."

"Oh yes, I knew that," she replied, when she clearly had not known. The conversation slowed to a stop as she stared at the water.

I still didn't know if she remembered visiting Maui before. The memories of us with the girls were long gone for her. And sometimes it had been just the two of us on vacation and that, too, seemed lost. But in fact, it was okay on this trip. I didn't care about missing memories, and I certainly wasn't about to get depressed on Maui. We got into swimsuits and hung out on the lawn at the condo, or waded into the ocean.

I have a picture from that trip; Jan is beaming with the smile that changes her whole face. She is standing in her swimsuit near the beach, happy in the hot sun. By the time I took the picture she had figured out where we were and was in the moment. It didn't matter if that moment would be lost as the next moment came along. It was enough that she was happy right then.

And it was here, for whatever unforgivable reason, that I would lose my temper with her. And when the dam broke, I couldn't stop myself.

It started because, as always, we wanted to look at real estate. An agent took us to see some houses on the hills above the town of Lahaina, where New England whaling ships once pulled in after their kills in the nearby waters where the whales would come to winter with their young. The houses on the hill were lovely. We liked one or two in particular and decided to have the agent drive us back for a second look. I was in my Maui uniform, a swimsuit and t-shirt, how Hawaiian, right? Since I didn't have pockets, I put the keys to the rental car in Jan's purse and put my wallet in the trunk of the rental car. We left the car parked at the condo complex and took off with the agent.

We saw several houses that day before the agent dropped us back at our condo. We were back for only a few minutes when I asked Jan for the car keys. "They're in your purse," I said matter-of-factly.

"Okay," she said. Then the ominous words from her, "Where is my purse?"

How could she not have her purse? She had never, not once, either lost her purse or gone out without one. I figured it was tucked away somewhere in the condo where she put it when we got back. "Where is it?" I repeated. We looked around. It doesn't take long to search a one-bedroom condo. No purse. "But you had it when we left," I pointed out, "because I put the car keys into it."

"I guess."

Maybe it was being tired from jet lag, maybe it was being tired from coping with the constant forgetfulness, but I got angry. Gritting my teeth, I said, "Darling, we can't go anywhere because the car keys are in your purse."

She stared at me and said nothing. There was nothing in her eyes that showed if she even understood. I started working the phones. Our real estate agent had caught a plane to a different island. No help there. I called the listing agent of one house we visited and where I suspected Jan left her purse. No luck there, either, since all I got was her voice mail. I then called the car rental agency, which was located at the airport on the other side of the island. Was there another set of keys, by chance? No. And there was a fee for making a new key because, these days, keys aren't cut at the local hardware store while you wait. They are electronic and it costs to have a new one programmed for a particular car. And how to get it to me . . . would they deliver the keys? Hawaiian hospitality ended at that point. No, they would not. They would give any new key to a cab driver who would bring it to me, but it would cost about a hundred dollars in cab fare.

I hung up and tried calling a local locksmith. Didn't people still do this? Yes, but for modern cars with electronic keys it takes time to get the codes, and it will be expensive and the rental car agency may not like a non-original key. But this was just a Ford, dammit. Can't people make a quick ordinary key for an ordinary damn Ford?

No.

Another try at the listing agent. Another request to leave a voice mail. Through it all, through this onslaught of people telling me what they couldn't do, Jan stood quietly in the kitchen, impassive. There wasn't a flicker of recognition that we were spending a precious afternoon of vacation not at the beach or relaxing, but dealing with car keys, and it was going to get pricey.

It was her impassivity and unawareness of what was going on that pushed me over the edge. I lost it. I don't remember ever shouting at her before, but I shouted now. "Don't you understand? We can't go anywhere! And my wallet is in the trunk, and that means we have no money or credit cards. We can't even buy groceries or go to dinner or buy a sandwich because every penny is in the wallet. Don't you get it . . . don't you see what you did?"

I look back at this with shame because I was yelling at her when she had no idea what she had done, and no ability to understand my anger. Instead, she stared back with no emotion. My words are burned onto my soul. It was the rage I had always directed at others, but never at her. How could I blame her for something she hadn't done and for something that terrified her? What kind of person had I become?

I close my eyes now and can still hear her scared, shaking voice from the early days of The Disease. "I'm losing my mind, aren't I?" I heard it then, too, even as my anger exploded. How could I be so angry? She hadn't done this on purpose. She was barely aware of what she had done. Maybe not even aware.

I reached down somewhere deep and calmed down before calling the rental car company, where I ordered the new key and had a taxi bring it across the island. About ninety minutes later, the taxi showed up. I was handing over a hundred dollar bill for the cab fare when my cell phone rang. It was the listing agent. She was sorry, she'd accidentally put her phone in the trunk of her car and missed my calls. A quick call to the people in the house and, yes, they had the purse. She offered to come pick us up.

In the end, it was a simple mix-up easily fixed, even if I was out a hundred bucks. I looked down at my new hundred-dollar replacement key and said to the agent, "thanks, but I can get there in my car." Jan and I drove back to the house, where the couple graciously handed over Jan's purse.

At this point, Shakespeare would say: "All's well that ends well." But it wasn't. How could I reach the point of being so frustrated that my anger erupted and I turned it on Jan? I wondered whether I was now the sick one, the one without perspective, the one whose emotions were so raw that I attacked the one person least able to understand, let alone know enough to even say, "I'm sorry, darling," because she had no idea why I was so furious.

For the rest of the week, even as I helped her relax in the surf or go out for lunch or dinner, I could still hear me shouting at her . . . "Don't you understand?" . . . and from farther back, from a moment of her still having awareness and fear, her words . . . "I'm losing my mind, aren't I?"

I was the one she trusted most, the one she needed most. What had I become?

TIMELINE
April, 2008
Barry's update to family and friends: Written two weeks before placing Jan into assisted living

Dear friends,

I hope at the end of this I can tell you of Jan being happy. There are no guarantees. To those who know her and love her – or even those who simply cherish her because she is always so bright in our lives – you already know that we are losing her. And now we have come to a new moment. Except for a rare few of her family and friends which I will explain, she is soon gone from you.

In early May we will move Jan into an assisted living facility. And, once there, this may be her home for the rest of her life. The facility is in Bellevue, WA, a metropolis of its own next to Seattle. She was raised here almost all her life. Her mom and most of her brothers and sisters are here, along with friends going back to college days. This is a good thing.

I came here to find a place and make the arrangements. She does not know about this. She will not be traveling with me anymore, as it is too confusing for her. I am told that I should not even take her to California or Hawaii or anywhere because it will leave her distraught and confused about where she is and where she lives.

This confusion is a major reason we need to settle her now. I have been saying goodbye to Jan in small ways for some time. Now, with little warning, she is physically leaving me and most of you will likely never see her again.

Jan will be living in a lovely two-room apartment, with huge windows on two walls of a ten-foot-high ceiling living room. As you know, she loves light and even on gloomy days this room is lit and cheerful and looks out onto the front veranda. It will be painted her favorite light pink/salmon color, and we will decorate it with favorite antiques and art work from Asia. Our goal is that when she looks around she will always see things familiar and cheerful and, being Jan, most will be BRIGHT red and gold.

Why now? In no particular order, here are some of the reasons. We have a wonderful live-in caregiver, Diane Malone, who works hard trying to get Jan out and about and stimulated with activities. Jan now sees Diane as the enemy and proof of her illness, and is increasingly defiant about going out with Diane or even talking with her.

You may remember previous notes about the afternoon Anger Monster. Now this anger at Diane is starting at breakfast and sometimes lasting all day through dinner. As hard as it is for Diane and me to cope with this, it is way too hard for Jan feeling this emotional upheaval all day.

Second, we think this is a good time for the transition because she is still aware enough to help out and be part of the process, if she so chooses and we make it work.

Third, and this is the reason I hate most of all, Diane and others around me are warning that I am now being dragged down in ways which will start affecting my health and well being, if it hasn't already. This is not unusual for caregivers, and studies show that being an Alzheimer's caregiver to a loved one can shorten your life rather dramatically.

I am not a hero and I do not think this situation is about me, because the focus is and must remain Jan. But I am also just barely smart enough that when it is pointed out, I can and do see what is happening to me, such as my deepening level of exhaustion or the effects of living on a never-ending emotional roller coaster. I am reliably informed that if I do not make this change, and soon, this will not end well for me. And while that is secondary to me because in this battle we must all put Jan first, there is logic to knowing that if I falter and fail she will suffer for it.

PLEASE DO NOT TALK TO JAN ABOUT ANY OF THIS if you call. We are crafting the ways to make the transition work and the critical issue is how and when we present this to Jan. She needs to hear this from me and I need to tell it in the right way. Even that is no guarantee she will accept it.
~Until then . . . Barry

14

"When you come to the end of your rope, tie a knot and hang on."
~Franklin D. Roosevelt

Into Assisted Living

It was spring in Tokyo, feeling warmer and better each day. Spring also brings the pleasure of cherry blossoms. The Japanese use the few weeks that the blossoms are in bloom as an excuse for late night parties beneath the pink flowering trees. Sometimes it is large groups, usually from the same company, having an evening picnic with beer and laughter and music. The best cherry blossom trees in Tokyo decorate the calm of cemeteries.

Planting the fragile cherry blossoms in a place devoted to death is a perfect place for the Japanese. To them, the cherry blossom season is about remembering the hardest lesson of human life — almost no one knows when life ends.

Life and cherry blossoms are incredibly fragile. The blossoms last a few weeks at best and some years harsh rainstorms and high winds will strip the trees bare while the blossoms are still in their prime. Even in good years, the blossoms are here briefly and gone. They are, the Japanese will tell you, a metaphor for life — enjoy them in the moment.

Japan cheers up during cherry blossom season. On the evening news, there are regular reports including maps showing the progression of the trees blooming starting in the south where it warms up first. If you live in Tokyo, you can watch and anticipate when the trees will flower in the metropolis.

The cherry blossom season of 2008 was a calm and enjoyable time. Jan was resting in the bedroom when Diane and I sat down to talk. Diane's try at a smile contrasted sharply against the late afternoon sun as it poured soft amber light into our Tokyo apartment. Maybe, she said gently, it was time to think about what we might need to do next. It was somewhere in her conversation that I first heard the words "Assisted Living."

In truth, I didn't recoil. Perhaps my reaction was worse - a sense of relief. Was there a way out of the endless day into night into day of my life? Diane had been with us only seven months, and in that time she could see the changes unfolding that I was missing. I had questions, and the most important was the hardest to answer. "How do we know that now is the right time?"

"It could be too soon," Diane admitted. "But if so, it's better if we do this when Jan is still able to adjust to a new place, and it will also help the staff get to know and bond with her if her personality is intact."

Jan, up from her nap, wandered into the living room and asked what we were talking about. I couldn't tell her. Instead, I smiled. "We were just talking about what to have for dinner." The next day, I booked a flight to Seattle to begin what I knew was the beginning of the end, the chapter where I would lose not only the woman I loved, but her presence in my daily life, and mine in hers. No need to come home cheerful because soon there would be no one there when I came home. And behind that thought was the unanswerable question out there . . . why come home at all?

Diane had a friend in Tacoma, WA who specialized in helping people like me find a place for people like Jan. Pat Ness was also a nurse, and her consulting firm, Elder Pathways, Ltd., proved to be perfect because of her focus on assisting elders and their families with their caregiving needs. Even though she smiled a lot, there was hard, sad experience beneath the surface, and a strength I opted never to challenge. I was glad she was on my side. She became my guide in the hunt for Jan's new home, helping me find the right assisted living facility and preparing me for this new phase of Jan's life and what I considered all but the end of mine.

I pushed that last part aside, thinking I would deal with it later, and later it came back to almost destroy me. But that was later. We tromped into and out of several places from Seattle to Tacoma. Every place we visited left me in shock with what was yet another lesson unique to Early Onset Alzheimer's. These were places for very old people in their seventies or eighties or 90s. None was geared for a bright, active woman in her late fifties.

And they knew it. Over and over again, I asked the director of this place or marketing manager of that one, how Jan would fit in with people so much older, and there was no real answer. They had little or no experience with having someone this young in their facility. I worried that Jan would see through the bright colors and lovely dining rooms and cozy small apartments and realize that she was living in a different world . . . the world of the aged and infirm.

There was no real choice. This is where people who need help with Alzheimer's often go while they are still functional. And most did not get The Disease until they were significantly older. We had odd moments along the way, like the food pitch. It seemed that each facility, according to whoever was selling us on the place, had its own dining room and tried giving the impression that French chefs would be envious of the amazing lunch and dinner dishes served on a daily basis.

I finally asked Pat what was up with all the emphasis on food? She explained how in times past there had been scandals about the poor or even disgusting quality of food given to residents in these old-age facilities. Now the good ones touted tasty food and attractive dining rooms. One had a dining room that felt like you were on a cruise ship. And with Alzheimer's, food is even more important because meal times are a critical part of setting routine. Most places did, indeed, have different selections for meals but each also had regular, constant choices like a turkey sandwich or hamburger.

The reason for that was people who have difficulty making choices can settle on one thing and order it at each and every meal if need be. I didn't get it then, but I did when Jan started doing just that. Unable to cope with a choice between two lunch selections, she would go for the hamburger almost every time with a sense of relief.

When we finally visited a facility in Bellevue, Jan's home town, it clicked. The one-bedroom apartment was perfect. It was on the first floor with big windows in the living room overlooking the roofed porch with outdoor easy chairs. It felt like looking across the veranda of a Southern plantation house. There was a lot of light, and Jan always responded well to the light.

It had a separate bedroom where most units were one room studios. In truth, Jan may not have cared about the difference between living in a single room and having the extra space of a small apartment, but I cared. I wanted something nice.

I created a small e-mail group called "Jan's Team" of close friends and family who lived in the immediate area. The idea was sharing among ourselves any day-to-day problems that we could work on together. This is from one of my first notes to "Jan's Team" just before we made the transition from Tokyo to Bellevue.

> I started talking with Jan this weekend about "our" moving to Bellevue. It was framed, as several of you had suggested, as the beginning of us moving home for good. I also said the idea of Bellevue was good at the moment because she has her mom, brothers and friends. She is actually getting enthusiastic about this. I think she is ready to go home, ready to be someplace with good and familiar friends, and surrounded by people who speak English.
>
> I have decided, as much as one can decide these things, to view this in a truly positive and, frankly, upbeat way. None of us can change the course of what is happening to her. But all of us working together can make her happy, and being in one place, having some stability, surrounded by normalcy and friends, is now the way to make that happen. So let us be glad that there is a good place for her and let's focus on making it a wonderful place.
>
> This is a journey I have never made. I am now less scared and more confident about the good we can do for Jan because of all of you.

I wanted to be comfortable that she was in a good facility. I wanted to look back whenever I left after a visit, knowing she was in a lovely space. And to prepare her lovely space, I enlisted help. One of her close friends from her local TV days, a fellow reporter with Jan, walked me through furniture stores and helped me pick out chairs and end tables and a bed. Then we went to the local paint store for samples of pink—"Jan Pink"—that we took to the apartment and decided which one worked, and then had the assisted living facility paint her apartment in that color.

I printed a dozen different photos of Jan with her parents, her brothers and sisters and her favorite aunt, of our wedding, of vacations we took with the girls. Another friend got them framed in different sizes and then went in ahead of us and spread them around the apartment as memory cues. To hang on the walls or decorate the tables, I brought an Asian-themed Buddhist wall hanging, pictures of Paris and London, a large antique Russian samovar (for boiling water to make tea) that we had smuggled out of the old Soviet Union. More memory cues. We did this before Jan set foot in the place because Pat and Diane warned me it could be a struggle getting Jan settled. I wanted to prepare by having as much around her as I could that was familiar.

She loved the apartment, but quickly and thoroughly hated the rest of the place. It started the moment she first walked in. "It's full of old people," she said.

I tried shrugging it off. "I'm sure they're nice and have amazing stories to tell." Fat chance.

"They're old. Old! I am not old. What are we doing here?"

I stayed with her the first few days and it tore at me because I felt the same way. I would walk with her into the dining room for meals and we would be the kids of the place, surrounded by many in wheelchairs or walkers or just struggling to get to a table. They were gray haired, Jan was blonde. They moved slowly, Jan was a ball of energy. It wasn't good, and it would never get better.

It would have been so much easier for her if there had been a place full of people her age, but there wasn't. Alzheimer's may be the coming fate of aging boomers and that means growth in the number of assisted living facilities, but not yet. And especially missing are places geared to those with Early Onset.

As for timing of the move, Diane was right . . . and wrong. It helped that Jan was more aware because she could adapt and could understand that this was "temporary" as part of "us" moving back to America. Yet, it also meant Jan sensed that something was fundamentally untrue about the story of moving back, that she was being forced into "living with the oldies." Like having a caregiver with us in Asia, this was another sign that she was ill.

More and more, as she faded, she insisted more firmly that she was fine. No Alzheimer's for her, and even getting her to take the medications was becoming a struggle. "I'm healthy as a horse," was her mantra. And her rock-solid insistence from the early days on taking her pills to fight The Disease turned into an attitude of angry resistance. Someone as healthy as a horse doesn't need pills!

By now, she was very adept at compensating, pretending she knew what was going on around her, when she clearly did not. Our friend, Kit Yarrow, got a taste of this.

She visited Jan in the summer of 2008, during Jan's first year in the facility. "Jan's gushy, girly love was the same," Kit said, "but she wasn't."

Jan didn't remember Kit, something hard for everyone when they visited and Jan clearly did not know who they were. But Jan's personality still came through.

"She greeted me," Kit told me, "with that huge red-lipped smile and pretended that she knew who I was, so she wouldn't offend me. In no time, we were sitting on a bench having a giggly, exuberant girl talk."

My focus was on her comfort, but there was also the reality of paying for these people to take care of her. In this, I had a touch of luck, and at this point I needed it badly. A decade earlier, we got a solicitation from AARP, the American Association of Retired Persons, offering an insurance company's long term disability policy that AARP recommended. I decided to buy it, thinking that I was someone fairly likely to take a bullet while on assignment and not wanting to become a burden to anyone. And because Jan and I did everything together, I bought a policy for her.

But having a paid-up policy did not guarantee payment. The insurance company assigned a case manager who began the process. She was initially dubious about Jan's needing this level of care at her age, for which they would have to pay.

Her care was going to cost about $6,000 a month. I hadn't figured out how to pay for this if the insurance company balked, except to begin selling things as fast as possible. I had this vision of the 1800s sternwheeler riverboat racing down the Mississippi River and running low on fuel, so the crew starts taking the boat apart plank by plank, feeding the wood into the boiler to keep going. That was the extent of my plan. Sell and scrimp.

The case manager was a nurse who talked with Diane as part of her assessment. Diane, out of professional habit, had kept notes on Jan's deterioration during her months in Asia. I remember the call from the insurance case manager; I had just pulled out of the parking lot of the facility onto a side street when the cell phone rang. When I answered and heard the voice of the case manager, I pulled over and parked assuming she needed more information and I would need to take notes. "Okay," I said, "go ahead."

"Mr. Petersen, I am calling to tell you that we have approved your claim."

There was more, about when the payments would start and needing to certify the facility and other details. I thanked her, hung up, stepped out of the rental car, walked around to the passenger side, leaned over with my hands on the roof, and began sobbing. It was equal parts relief and joy, that something—anything—about this part of Jan's care was finally working out.

The insurance covered up to about $5,000 of the monthly expenses. But with the extras that Jan needed, the bill was closer to $6,000 so I paid about $1,000 a month out of my pocket. But this wasn't the end of it. I was warned that as Jan's condition worsened and she needed a higher level of care, my out of pocket costs would increase because the insurance reimbursement was at its maximum. So while the basics were covered, the extras, which meant her extra care, would only go higher.

I shuddered to think about what if the insurance company had said no, or I had no insurance. How would I have paid the roughly $72,000 a year? I still don't know. It's yet another cost of The Disease when it strikes early. Jan was too young for Medicare, which in most cases doesn't cover assisted living anyway. She was fifty eight when I placed her into the facility. And because of The Disease, she was unable to work much in

those last years, so she didn't pay enough into Social Security to
qualify for disability. No help there.

I felt lucky, because for some without insurance, there is a
terrible other option—divorce. Without assets, the patient
qualifies for Medicaid. Some people who have been married for
decades have to go through this. The reason is that if they stay
married and the government pays the bills, it will go after the
surviving spouse for repayment. That means a surviving spouse
can face tens of thousands of dollars in bills and must, by law,
sell off virtually everything they own to pay off the "debt." It
leaves people destitute.

Do they spend all the savings once earmarked for a child's
college education, or money that was put aside for just plain
living? This is not that rainy day covered by that nest egg. This is
the Biblical flood that can wipe out everything.

Once she moved in, there were other problems and one of
the first was about her clothes. I packed suitcases of clothes for
her when we came from Tokyo in my desire to give her a variety
of outfits. Instead, she would open her closet and stand, unable
to decide among so many clothes. So one day, when Jan went to
lunch, I had someone go into her apartment and take away
almost all of her beautiful clothes. Left behind were the black
jeans she always wore, the black cashmere sweaters and her
pajamas. It ended her confusion about the simple but difficult act
of deciding what to wear. All part of the ongoing fine tuning.

Listening to those with experience and following their
advice made me confident that I had done it right. I didn't. I
misjudged one fundamental truth of Alzheimer's and its never-
ending way of playing tricks with Jan's brain. The Disease
would sometimes let her vibrant personality burst through, and
that convinced some of her friends that I was anything but a
loving husband and caregiver. Some were convinced I had let
Jan down, that I had acted in all the wrong ways. And the
hardest accusation of all was that I didn't love Jan. And worse;
that I was purposely hurting her by moving—some said
dumping her—into this facility. In their eyes, I was a man whose
actions bore the mark of betrayal.

TIMELINE
June, 2008
Barry's update to family and friends

I am sorry that some of you are angry with me for putting Jan into assisted living. I should have anticipated that, and I didn't. I forgot that I have lived with this for years, and you are just now coming face to face with this baffling, unpredictable illness. This is a deceptive, wily disease that is attacking someone articulate and charming and beautiful.

I happily took care of Jan myself, and in time that didn't work. I got friends involved to make sure she was okay when I traveled, and in time that didn't work. I hired a live-in caregiver, flew her halfway around the world and even rented her an apartment for when we were in Beijing because the flat there is too small, and in time that didn't work.

If you need to be angry with me, I accept that. I have and will continue to make my decisions based solely on what I believe is best for Jan. And I also know that much of your anger with me is truly about what Jan is going through, about her confusion and anxiety, about how this seems so bloody unfair.

We are now at a moment when we can make Jan comfortable, content and mentally stimulated in her new home, and she gets to spend time with all of us. And these things could actually help her get better.

This is a very delicate time in the transition. We have a chance – and NO guarantees here despite our good intentions – to get this right. Jan is amazing. She is by nature upbeat, happy, vivacious. And we are a dream team, believe me. Think how, together, we span all the parts of her life. She is so blessed to have people like you, and she has you because of who she is and how wonderful and fun and adventurous she is.

We can still have that Jan but ONLY if we, together, make this delicate transition work in the weeks ahead. Or we can, singly or as a group, blow it for her. And the result of that is too sad to contemplate.
~Best . . . Barry

15

"Those who mind don't matter and those who matter don't mind."
~Dr. Seuss

The Evil They Say Is Me

I was on the northern California coast, sipping morning coffee, looking across a field toward the ocean, when the cell phone rang.

"Why have you abandoned her?" It was one of Jan's oldest friends, her fury laced with venom. "You don't love her. If you really loved her, you would be there right now and taking care of her."

I had just come from being with Jan at the assisted living facility and was taking a few days for myself to sit quietly and be alone in an empty house to listen to the sound of the waves. I needed a mental recess, an emotion-free period, before heading back to work in Asia. No such luck.

"You abandoned her." For twenty minutes she told me how I did not, could not really love Jan. True love, she yelled, meant giving up everything, including my job, and moving to where Jan was and being with her every day that she had left and helping take care of her no matter Jan's condition. Or, by implication, no matter my condition.

And then, just as abruptly, she said she had an appointment and hung up. My entire contribution to the conversation had started and ended with "Hello." Even if she had made time to listen or wanted to hear me, what would I say? I thought I had done it right. I had reached out to experts. I had found a wonderful place for Jan to live, and now I was being portrayed as a man who had betrayed the woman whose only fault was that she loved me.

As a caregiver, I appreciated sympathy. It helped. But when the days were hardest, what I really needed was understanding.

Understanding meant people accepted and supported what I was doing. They got it. When you are grasping and, in my case, too often stumbling uncertainly for a way forward, acceptance and support help beat back the doubts and the confusion.

To understand, people need to see what you see. And this is where my inexperience led to a terrible miscalculation. Jan's friends and family could not see what I had been seeing day-to-day because Jan and I were five thousand miles away. Unlike Diane and me, they had not been through the ever-tougher daily battles and the anger or the withdrawal, or watched her struggle with a horrible confusion just trying to find the words for a sentence. I thought I was making it clear in the updates to family and friends how fast Jan was changing.

I plotted the move into assisted living as carefully as I could, assuming everyone would understand why this was a crucial way of helping Jan. And just as I was patting myself on the back thinking the transition was working, I slammed head-on into that wall of anger and disapproval. I didn't factor in the brightness of Jan shining through. How funny that one of the things that made me first love her, and something she still mercifully had, now made others basically distrust and detest me.

They saw a Jan who was still cheerful and beautiful. That is how The Disease works. It doesn't distort the body, and it can leave some traits alive, like Jan's smile and laughter. If you aren't there at the bad moments, if you aren't there to agonize over another sign of deterioration, you couldn't see how much she had changed. Instead, you only see the person you remembered, as if all of her were still there.

And, in that kind of denial, all you'd see is this lovely person who did not deserve being "placed" in a "facility." And you could detest the man who did it. These friends didn't want to see the Jan who had a terminal disease or see that we would lose more of her each day. Instead, they focused on a husband who (in their eyes, and maybe they were right?) had bungled watching over her these last few years, and then had hired a live-in caregiver who irritated Jan, and finally had moved with too much haste to "dump" her into a "warehouse" where she was being sentenced to a form of life imprisonment.

I didn't blame them. I had the same doubts and a sense of guilt about leaving her where I could not watch over her, could not help her in the days and nights. But someone had to make this call because it was coming sooner or later, and I was it.

Now I was at a critical moment, the moment of making this transition work. Jan needed the routine of the facility to help her through the day. She needed nurses and staff watching over her, people cooking for her, and friends who visited in what I hoped would become an always-familiar and, for her, safe place that would ease her confusion.

If she could have these things, then she could have a form of peace that I was unable to give her by shuttling us between Tokyo and Beijing, or even by having a live-in caregiver. With this constant traveling, she was increasingly lost in confusion. And that confusion fed her anger, and seeing her angry and unhappy made me feel like a dismal failure of a husband and a caregiver.

As Alzheimer's progresses, it is harder for the person to add new information. That is why routine is so critical. Jan needed to wake up in the same bedroom at the same time and have the same chair at the same table at mealtimes with the same people. Change means readjusting and that is one thing we needed to avoid.

I imagined her Alzheimer's at this point as like a person watching a movie and, as it goes along and new information keeps being added, it speeds up the movie. It's like someone is pushing the fast-forward button, making it faster and faster and, in time, it is incomprehensible because the images are flashing by so quickly you can't even make them outandthewordsaregibberishthatcantbeunderstood.

Finally, the person simply shuts down, closing their eyes and mind to the too-fast movie and withdraws. And this is repeated every day. The movie starts and then speeds up as the day unfolds and finally the mental chaos is overwhelming and then . . . shut down.

The point of making her surroundings familiar and routine was to make it less challenging for her mind. I wanted to keep the movie running at normal speed. This was what Jan badly needed now, and I thought everyone would see it as I did. I was wrong.

It was hard for her mom. Caron had spent several years caregiving for her wonderful husband, and he had just died. I expected that she, above all others, would understand the need for Jan to be someplace safe and normal and routine. She didn't at first. She was among the doubters who grew into being what I called "The Angry."

They had to see, and they could not see it from me. At least I got that part right. I organized what I called "The Intervention," a family gathering in Caron's living room where The Angry could face the experts. I would not be there because I was on the way back to Asia. The transition to assisted living was only a few days old, and it was already in disrepair. And worse, it was in danger of collapse. There were mutterings about moving Jan out of the facility. I was alarmed. How had I done such a bad job explaining Jan's condition and failed in getting people to understand my decision?

There was a threesome batting for my side; Dick, my Alzheimer's Buddy, Diane, and Jullie Gray, a social worker who helped in founding the medical ethics committee at a local hospital. I had just hired Jullie as a care manager and kind of ombudsman for Jan. She would watch over both Jan and the facility for me while I was in Asia, and help resolve any medical problems beyond what the facility staff could routinely handle.

"Diane and I had visited Jan at the assisted living facility before our meeting," Jullie told me later. "Jan was socially engaging but had significant language difficulties when I spoke to her. I quickly realized that if someone met her for the first time and wasn't knowledgeable about Alzheimer's disease, and if Jan was having a good day, she could appear very 'normal.' "

Jullie came to the intervention with charts and pictures and explained in graphic and uncompromising detail how Alzheimer's attacks, physically alters and destroys the brain. Jullie is a charming woman, bubbly and upbeat. But her tough, experienced, no-nonsense side made what she said all the more believable. She was teaching her version of Alzheimer's 101, because if you do not know The Disease and have not lived with it for years or decades, it can fool with ease. The first-timer rarely gets it right.

Gently and firmly Jullie explained The Disease and its tricks. "It's not unusual for people to initially believe that a person with Alzheimer's is more capable than he/she really is. Many times, family members will incorrectly attribute challenging behaviors to 'acting out' as if they were doing it on purpose, rather than as a result of the disease."

Jullie offered this from her own experience. "I've seen family members say, 'She knows what she's doing, and she's just trying to make me angry.' When a family member believes a person is more capable than he or she really is, the family member expects too much of the person with Alzheimer's and gets incredibly frustrated."

Jullie came with pictures, showing how the brain changes as the cells slowly die. She hoped that by showing Jan's family images of the physical alterations, they would understand that The Disease is real.

Diane, wisely, mostly stayed quiet because she sensed that the room was against her, especially since there was blunt talk of moving Jan out of the facility and into a regular apartment with a "good" caregiver. The implication was clear; Diane was the "bad" caregiver who had been difficult for Jan to be around and had prematurely encouraged my placing Jan. "From the get-go when walking in," Diane told me later, "my guard was up, as the hostility toward me was very apparent. Each time I spoke or attempted to explain why we made the decisions we did, I was cut off." Some of those in the room thought Diane had, in some way, brainwashed me into moving Jan, and in their eyes that was not the best thing for Jan.

And Dick, calm and solid, told how he had retired from his job to be the full-time caregiver for Dorothee after her diagnosis. His was the personal part of the story—the years caring for Dorothee and how he finally decided it was time for her to go into a facility. The timing, he told them, had as much to do with concerns about his health as much as hers.

Dick told them they should not judge me since they have not, and cannot, walk in my shoes. "Barry, you made the correct decision, and they needed to respect you for it."

He was the logical one to handle the question of "why didn't Barry just quit CBS News and move to Seattle and care for

Jan?" I am not sure I appreciated his answer, as he told me later, "Look at the reporters on local TV," he said. "There aren't very many old ones. It's mostly young ones, starting out in their careers. Or they had been in Seattle for years, long enough to have a firm hold on their positions. Do you think Barry could really get a TV job in Seattle these days?"

Not flattering, but true. I had a job which supported caring for Jan and if I gave it up, there might not be work for me in the immediate area, and CBS News had no office in Seattle.

Diane reinforced the point, and got a verbal boost from Jan's mom, Caron. "She came to my rescue, and suggested we take notice that the majority of new anchors were young, blond attractive women."

And Dick shared one more thing; how Dorothee's friends had dropped away as Alzheimer's took away more of her brain. "I still feel my sorrow that Dorothee's friends have abandoned her, and I told them about the hurt that I still feel over that."

The key focus of the intervention was explaining how The Disease tricks and steals, how it was possible for Jan to be bright and cheerful and stay that way for a while longer even as memories and competence slip away. The point was to drive home how critical routine was to Jan's well being. Routine could bring comfort, and the facility could provide that routine.

In the end, the intervention initiated the changing of minds . . . but only the beginning. Jan's old friend, who was angriest with me, stopped and talked with Jullie as the evening was winding down.

Jullie remembers it this way: "After the meeting, she (Jan's friend) sought me out in the kitchen for a private talk. She talked and I listened as empathetically as I could. She needed me to know and validate her relationship with Jan, and wanted to go over again how angry she was with you, Barry. I sensed that she needed to be able to express her anger before she could move anywhere else emotionally. She asked if she could call me for a private discussion, and I encouraged her to do so. I knew she wanted to 'get me on her side,' to see things the way she saw things. I tried to be neutral, to listen, really listen, and hear her concern.

"I felt that she was going through the normal grieving process and she was stuck in 'anger' for the moment. She hadn't had as much time to get to the place of accepting Jan's disease, and I hoped with time, she would be able to get there."

That was the key . . . the grieving. The Disease makes no space for closure, no moment of knowing that a life is over. Instead, it robs slowly and softly. And that meant the people around Jan, seeing her as she settled in, had a terrible choice that I already knew all too well; accept or reject that Jan was terminally ill.

Rejecting comes more naturally. I understood this. I spent years doing just that. How foolish of me to think that others would skip this phase. They, too, needed time to find their grief and then acceptance, even as Jan still stood alive and lovely and lively in front of them.

Their suspicion of my motives remained, along with the anger. It took time — months, in fact — for attitudes to soften and for insight to replace accusation. And for some, there was no softening, and may never be.

In those first weeks of transition for Jan there was so much emotion because they didn't want to see Jan leaving us; or if they did see it, then they needed to blame something or someone for the changes in this lovely woman we all cherished. That someone was me. I can talk about it now with detachment, but I couldn't at the time. I was crushed.

It was bad enough for me that the decision was driven in part because my exhaustion as a caregiver was rapidly getting worse and endangering my health, leaving me feeling that I had somehow failed Jan. That exhaustion also meant I plowed into this transition with no reserve of emotional strength.

And it was bad enough that Jan and I were losing our everyday life together. Yes, life with Jan in Asia was difficult and getting worse fast, but at least it included her being there with me. Now, for her good, I had to give her up to an assisted living facility. Was this not love, was this not sacrifice? Was this not enough, dammit? Can't I be left alone with my private agony? Can you understand, and not judge me?

The disapproval and anger scratched across already-bleeding nerves. Over and over, I checked back with the people I had consulted and trusted, and they assured me that putting Jan into the facility was exactly what she needed at this stage. But I was already feeling despair, and adding to the pain were the accusations that I was abandoning her, or I had done something to purposely hurt her. That swelled my despondency into something I could physically feel in my gut.

And inside me, there was another storm of emotion forming; without Jan, why keep going? Why? It is a volatile and dangerous question. And when there seems no purpose and no destination in life, there looms a dark place where there is an answer, a frightening but calmly appealing answer. And I thought perhaps in that darkness I would find, if not solace, an end to the pain.

TIMELINE
November, 2008
Barry's update to family and friends

Dear All,

For a long time I have talked about losing Jan. Now, Jan is losing me. During my visit with her last week there were several moments, I don't know how many, when she did not know who I was while I was actually with her. And if I left for an hour or so, she forgot I was even in town seeing her. And after I left to visit my daughters living in Denver, she was angry that I never came to see her. She had no memory of my visit.

People who are wise and more experienced than I say this is part of the progression of The Disease. And, of course, they are right. But it leaves my soul in ashes. I don't know what to write because I don't know what to think or feel. Throughout all of our married togetherness, I proudly protected and nurtured Jan, and she did the same for me. There is not a "thing" that she wanted for us that I didn't get for her and it enriched our lives, and not a pain or torment that I suffered on stories or in life that she could not soothe and finally heal when I could come home to her.

When I married Jan I knew that I would never be alone, and I vowed that she would never be without me watching over her. Now there she is, still sparkling as you all remember her, yet increasingly unable to speak sentences that make any sense and leaving us for some other place.

And how do I live with a loneliness made worse because of what we once were? I am drifting without her. Drifting to what or where, I do not know. There is a sense that men have about protecting the people they most love. My list is pretty short . . . Jan, my two daughters, my granddaughter. But I could not protect Jan and now cannot stop or even slow what is going on. I feel powerless and helpless and, yes, finally, useless.

There are moments when I feel such intense failure that I simply freeze in place and wonder about just getting up and going on. Why bother? If I couldn't take care of Jan, what really was my life all about?

And worse, do I really want the "rest of my life" like this? The rational, intellectual part of all of us says this is not to be taken so personally. I didn't cause this, and I am not making it worse.

But the heart of me feels that she depended on me to care and protect her, and I failed. And as I watch her slip away, there is no atonement and no forgiveness for this failure.

Here are a few glimpses from our visit. When I was in her apartment with the TV on, I would find her staring at me. This seemed odd to me, until other events helped me realize that these may have been moments when she was trying to place me.

She was concerned one night about my coming back to the assisted living facility because having a strange man in her apartment might be viewed as a bit . . . racy?

As I write this, I am sitting in our house in northern California. Everywhere I look inside there is Jan, in the paintings or art she picked, in the pink walls that soothe when you sit here. She drove almost two hours each way to the paint dealer, three or four times, before she found the exact mix of color she wanted for this house. They actually saved the mix formula and filed it for future reference under "Jan's Pink."

Outside the house, it is a winter's day. There is heavy mist and fog. I can see waves close to the house, but as you look far away the world is nothingness. Out there is the unknown, the abyss. Is that where I will soon be without her?

~ Barry

16

"If you do not change direction, you may end up where you are heading."
~Lao-Tzu

Alone in the Darkness

The nights were the worst.

Sometimes, in that confusion between asleep and awake, I would sense her next to me. I could hear her breathing and actually feel her in the bed, feel her on the mattress next to me. Then I would wake up and she was gone and I would know, again, that I was alone.

I would tell myself that I will be alone from now on. It is like some lesson that I already knew but my mind keeps teaching and reminding me. I didn't understand why.

I had been alone all of my life—children of alcoholics often feel like that—until the moment Jan and I decided we were to be together. And in that moment, and because of her, the feeling of being alone went away. With Jan in my life I did not have to live in some separate place. Could I shout this joy to anyone who would listen, could I celebrate it, could I treasure the moments and savor each new day?

And then over the years doctors and friends and even my own daughters tried to show me that I was losing her. Could I stay sane? But the real question was, why bother? I knew I was in trouble when the therapist in Beijing who had helped me with Post Traumatic Stress Disorder gave me his vacation contact phone number and told me to call if needed. We had been talking about suicide. Mine.

I had written the November update which alarmed family and friends. Some tried calling the night they got it, convinced that I was preparing to kill myself. Perhaps they were right. I was finally and hopelessly lost in the darkest part of a valley, a deep abyss, a place that offers no good reason to go on. In this valley, in this blinding blackness, all you can see is what is gone. And you only see that in your memories.

Have not each of us wandered, from time to time, into that valley? When you look up, there is no light. The future has no shape, no reality. What alarmed the therapist in Beijing was my calm and casual description of ways I planned my demise. There was the slitting wrist in the bathtub plan, with the hot water somehow soothing the pain. There was jumping, of course. This would be easy because I lived in Tokyo on the 26th floor of a building with two balconies. I just had to step over the railing. It seemed messy, I explained to him, and really not for me. And how awful if you changed your mind on the way down. What then?

I said that at times, when holding a knife and slicing something, I considered how easy it would be to use that on myself and stab out, cut out the pain. It was the pain, not my life that I wanted to end. But they were twisted together in my body.

Because I lived in China and Japan, I did not have access to guns. There were empty, endless nights when I wished I had one. If there had been a gun in the apartment, I would have gotten it, stared at it, considered how fast and efficiently it would make the pain go away. One wonders what might have happened.

What do you ponder when you stand on the precipice? I felt that I would never again have what I had lost, that open and caring and unquestioned love she gave me. I got lucky, once. That was once more than a lot of people who I know. And what if the future stretched like it felt at that moment, from one dark restless pointless night to another? How many nights or days could I endure? Because, if I didn't actually kill myself, I would surely go insane. Which was better . . . or worse?

I would imagine myself being insane. One day they would miss me at work and someone would finally break into the apartment and I would be crouched in a corner, holding myself tightly. Do not touch me, do not help me, I would yell. Leave. Now! This is a future worth living? Dissolving into insanity? I didn't think so.

And then there was the wondering if I could have done anything else to have helped Jan. For years I read books and articles on Early Onset Alzheimer's Disease. Lots of people have lots of ideas about how and when it starts. No one knows for sure. I knew Jan's family had no known background of Alzheimer's. But did I do something; did I move her somewhere like Moscow with a toxic environment? And if not that, how about missing several years of symptoms when I could have done . . . what?

There is selfishness to suicide. The appeal is dimmed by the damage left behind. My daughters would cry. It would hurt them and they would wonder for years why I had done it. Hurting them is something I was never able to do. It is funny how a slender thread like that can pull you back. Just a tug, really, something on the edge of my mind saying that it would hurt the ones left behind, the ones I also care for, the innocents. And this time I would be the one hurting the innocents.

There was no moment of sudden wisdom, no jumping up and down and shouting that I was all for life. Had there been a moment like that, I wouldn't have trusted it. It was a slower, harder, inch-by-inch crawl back. I got through today, I did my job and I went home. I just had to do it again, tomorrow. Some days, most days, I would climb into bed and put a pillow over my eyes to shut out the light and the noise and find some comfort in the calm of darkness and silence.

There is no way to know if others saw any of this in me. I would like to think that they didn't because this seemed too raw, too human. I was falling to the bottom and trying to find my way back. And was it all the way back? No. Hidden underground were the landmines waiting for me, hiding in the days ahead. This I didn't know and could not anticipate. The Disease delights in agonies that devastate without warning. As it reached deeper into Jan's mind, erasing ever more parts of her, it reached into my gut and twisted sharp and hard.

And surely it couldn't get worse. Surely, The Disease would show some kind of mercy?

Walking Into Oblivion With No Exit: Stage Seven

This is the final stage . . . individuals lose the ability to respond to their environment, the ability to speak and, ultimately, the ability to control movement . . . frequently individuals lose their capacity for recognizable speech, although words or phrases may occasionally be uttered . . . individuals need help with eating and toileting and there is general incontinence of urine . . . individuals lose the ability to walk without assistance, then the ability to sit without support, the ability to smile, and the ability to hold their head up. Reflexes become abnormal and muscles grow rigid. Swallowing is impaired. (Seven Stages of Alzheimer's Disease from www.alz.org, the Alzheimer's Association)

As events moved ever faster and ever more beyond my control, I stopped and thought about what to do in the years ahead. I thought about the final stage. Even then it was hard to use that word . . . death.

It left me feeling the need to prepare for this last battle, to finally get one damn step ahead of The Disease. For once I was making contingency plans, or at least having contingency thoughts. I began wondering if the best course would be leaving my job and moving back to the US, taking Jan out of assisted living so we could live together again, and I would become her full-time caregiver. Who better?

Leaving my job would eliminate the stress and pressure from work and free me up for full-time caregiving, although it would also eliminate my salary. No one gets paid for staying home as a caregiver to the one you love. Listen to the laughter when you try that claim on the insurance company.

I would need to make the money part work if I didn't have my current job. Bills from mortgages to credit cards to heating the house don't evaporate because The Disease has come calling. I could do it if I just sold things. It could all go. And really, I thought, how much did I need to make her happy and give us a good life? A comfortable place to live, some wine, and sunsets would be enough. I could be there for her during the day and with her through the night.

And as I debated with myself about ending my career, that in itself became a new kind of denial; turning away from what was coming.

I was making a plan that had little to do with reality, because the last stage was the reality I would not face. So, I thought in the midst of this denial, if I upended what was left of my life and devoted myself to Jan, maybe there would be no last stage.

If I gave full-time to the war against The Disease, focused every part of myself and my energy, took Jan for long walks to keep her brain stimulated and kept her happy by just being with me because she was always happy when she was with me, then maybe I could finally make a difference and we could stop The Disease and I never have to face the last stage.

I picked up the phone and called a friend. Richard Leibner of NS Bienstock has also been my agent since my first days at CBS News and has carefully guided my career. I told him I was thinking of quitting and why I thought that would help Jan.

And he saw clearly what I didn't see at all. For a change, I listened. I was getting better at that. It was a late-night call for me from Tokyo and first thing in the morning for him in New York, as it always is when you are fourteen time zones away. I was really just thinking out loud about quitting.

And Richard said: "No."

No? Why not quit, I said? Why not give myself over to taking care of Jan? She had always taken care of me, loved me. It was my turn to give back. Why not?

Gently, because he is a temperate but very clear speaking man, he put it like this: "You will need something for when Jan is gone. You need to keep this job because you will need something to do for after."

With those words, he rocketed me from the misery of the present to the total loss coming, and that I would most likely still be alive after Jan passed through Stage Seven. Or be honest and call it after Jan's death caused by Early Onset Alzheimer's Disease.

He had ever so cautiously put into words what I would not even put into thought.

" . . . .you will need something . . . for after."

I apologized to Richard because I knew there were already tears in my eyes, and he graciously let me hang up. And then I sobbed. Jan was sick, she was leaving me, and we were losing to The Disease. My emotions that night were driven by panic and sadness and knowing that for the first time in my life I needed to begin thinking about what would be . . . after Jan.

I couldn't know how the years ahead would play out, and I didn't know what steps were yet to come. I hadn't done all that well to this point. I hadn't seen clearly that we would need a live-in caregiver and hadn't anticipated how that would ultimately fail and failure would force ever tougher decisions.

And if you had tried telling me what was coming that night, tried describing Jan's final stage, I would have swatted you away, fists flailing, trying to hurt you or push you away from me while tears streamed down my face. I couldn't hear it then, I wouldn't see it then. All I could see was that someday, Jan would be gone and I would be living alone in a place called "after."

There is nothing special about me. I have no overwhelming courage to survive and go on in spite of it all. Other people are like that, not me. I have met them and told their stories and admired them, but that isn't me, except for one ember of rage in my soul that would not go out. If I gave up, The Disease would have won. The Disease would have taken us both down.

And I didn't realize that my own life was also literally at stake. If I were a betting man, sitting at that desk, crying after the phone call that night and wondering if I could go on, I would have said . . . even odds.

Maybe less.

17

"It is not the strongest of the species that survives, nor the most intelligent that survives. It is the one that is the most adaptable to change."
~Charles Darwin

Where Am I Going

I am not a solitary person. This despite the million hours I think I've spent flying to and from stories, and the thousand nights alone in hotel rooms. But I didn't feel alone in those days because I had Jan to call and talk about what was happening, or how the story was going, or when I might make the flight I liked best, the one heading home and back to her. With Jan in my life, solitude was gone. And, in my mind, it would be gone forever.

Forever now had a termination date and it was time to realize that I could, as the proverb goes, curse the darkness and decide that is where I would live.

Or I could light a candle.

It was not an obvious choice, and my first instinct was to stay in the darkness. There was sadness there but also safety. Jan was all I had ever needed when she was with me, and I thought that I could live on in those memories. And maybe that was the new forever, the memories that would not fade even as Jan did.

There was also denial here, of not seeing how much Jan was changing, how fast she was going away from me. I did not and I could not admit that someday she would be completely gone. That was the forever that I could not face.

And then around me, with compassion that awes me still, were others who could see more clearly. They came to these conversations with me as only old friends can, with the courage to say what I didn't want to hear. They knew the love

Jan and I once had, and they understood its loss and they could see where I was eroding, where the sadness was hardening and might soon be all I had left. And they rejected that on my behalf.

But first they had to persuade me, and so they took the risk of showing me a way ahead. They took out a match and lit a candle and coaxed me out of the darkness before it consumed me.

By now I had stared down suicide. At times the thoughts would come back because it seemed such a simple solution, but each time with less force, less appeal. Even today, it sometimes whispers to me from the darkness. But surviving means moving forward. I have dealt with depression most of my adult life, and one form of relief is just moving, going for a walk, exercising, doing something physical that shakes up the body and gets the mind quite literally someplace else.

I can remember the first time a friend offered this kind of advice—to see a new way ahead. We were at lunch at a Manhattan restaurant. It was the fall of 2007. Mark Angelson and I first met when we both lived in London. He and his wife and daughters knew Jan. We went to their house for occasional festive events like Thanksgiving, when Americans tend to gather no matter where they are in the world. He was a successful lawyer who turned into an even more successful CEO and yet, he was a man with a gentle way and a quiet voice. He finds life fascinating and is one of the rare few who can find the lives of others equally fascinating and important.

And he took me aback with these words. "You need to find a woman."

In my mind I protested. I am married to Jan. She is the woman. At that point, we still lived together in Asia, although by now with the caregiver.

"Keep it light."

These were my immediate thoughts; being "light" was fair warning that I was in no way ready for deep emotions, commitment, or even love. It was too early, and I was dangerously vulnerable. But he knew that I needed some form of comfort now. It comes with being human. He was not really giving advice. He was offering permission, and he was the first to do so. I did not see what to him was clear; that being so alone was overtaking and defining my life and I was in misery without touch and caress.

I can remember his words, but not one of mine in reply. My emotions are what I recall. Could I do this? I did not leap to any moral high ground. I simply thought about going forward. Could I have this? Was this right? If the situation were reversed, would I want this for Jan? There is more to a man being with a woman than intimacy or ecstasy. There is life and vibrancy. He looked inside me and saw these feelings ebbing away.

After lunch I shook his hand and we said the things men say and I walked out into an easy New York autumn day carrying these thoughts. I was certain I could not do what he suggested, and yet there were others who echoed what Mark said. The ones who surprised me were old friends in northern California where I have a house. They have been happily married a long time. Together they created a very successful company. He was the man in front, who sold and created, and she was the partner in back, who sorted out books and plane flights and also created with him.

And they are still very much in love. You feel it when they are together, the kind of love only people who have been and built their lives together have. Yet they both, in the course of about five minutes, told me it was time to find someone new. This was a few months after I had placed Jan. From them, the couple who personified marriage and faithfulness, it was a shock. I had figured them for the "other side," the ones who thought I had abandoned Jan and didn't love her enough because I was not with her. They were wiser than I, as they have always been.

Patty is nurturing and caring of those she loves. She was sweet but clear. "You need to find someone." Her husband, Peter, is tall, blunt, and straightforward. He dominates any room he is in. He walked in, seconds after she finished, and just said it: "You should find someone."

They had obviously talked about it — they used almost the same words — and I was touched, if knocked a bit off balance.

They said this from almost twenty years of friendship and affection as strong for Jan as for me. Many times Jan and I had sat at their dinner table, often with others, and laughed and had wine. We argued the state of the union and always, always parted sorry that the evening was over.

I suspected others believed what they did. It made me uncomfortable on a number of levels. First, it seemed disloyal to even consider finding someone else. Jan had done nothing wrong in developing The Disease. She still remembered that she had a husband named Barry, or at least had a husband, although it was harder for her to recognize me in person when I was with her, or to remember I was there if I left the room for even a few minutes.

Second, was this my leaving her? Or was it finally a recognition that she was leaving me, despite all I had tried and done? The Disease can warp all sense of reality, and perhaps the reality that I didn't want to face was that she was gone.

Finally, who could replace her?

I knew there could never be another Jan. Perhaps someone else, someone different, but I was still aching for what had been. I was sure there were several who might be willing to take Jan's place in my life. There are a lot more women in my age range searching for friendship and companionship than there are men. But then I had to wonder why would someone want to try? Why take on a man who already has a wife, even if she was gone in so many ways? This is complicated, unknown. And as time went on, it would stay complicated. Jan was still healthy and I was still going to take care of her. If there was to be a new relationship, it had to be about we three . . . Jan, me and a new woman in my life. That was a lot to ask of anyone.

I had not lost the weight from the years of stress, caregiving, and seeing Jan fade. I didn't much care how I dressed. I was emotionally drained. My oldest daughter, Emily, put it rather too bluntly, but honestly. "Dad, you're not really a great catch." Not a confidence builder. Yet, there was truth in it.

Then there was something else, much harder, said to me by my Alzheimer's Buddy, Dick Lundgren. We had finished breakfast at a local hotel when I was visiting Jan in Bellevue. I was walking him to his car and we paused to chat in the parking lot. I asked him the question. "Will you ever have another relationship?"

He was quick to answer, and firm. "No."

"Why?"

I could see pain in his face as he struggled for a moment to get the answer right. "Because I couldn't go through this again."

"This" . . . was Alzheimer's. He had already sacrificed years fighting The Disease that had brought him, as he knew it would from the beginning, to being a man alone. There was no fight, no energy left inside him should he need to nurture and care for another woman who might, by some horrible coincidence, develop this kind of disease. What were the chances? Didn't matter, not the point. That it could happen was enough.

And yet, it didn't work out that way. Dick met someone and, in time, they discovered that they had much in common and, in time, they both realized that love can happen again. With courage, and one truly deep breath, he started over.

We, in this situation, are harbingers of what is coming upon society. There will be more and more who lose a loved one in mind and spirit while the body is still alive. That is because Alzheimer's cases are increasing. We are the Boomers, we live longer, and longer means more chances to develop Alzheimer's at fifty or sixty. Or seventy, the so-called new fifty.

Here is a prediction from the Alzheimer's Association: Today, every seventy seconds, someone in America develops Alzheimer's. By mid-century, someone will develop Alzheimer's every thirty-three seconds. So we, the survivors, don't know what we are, or how to act, or what the rules are.

Those who counseled me through the loneliness were people who saw what I couldn't. If asked, I said I was well and coping. I did all the right things to project the image of someone who is fine, and by the way, thanks for asking, just need to get over a few rough spots and work on that waistline, and isn't that just always the case.

I didn't know that even my own children saw it differently. Here is how Emily described me to someone else, "He's been very sad for a very long time now, longer than I think he even realizes." I understood about the sad part. Okay, I wasn't hiding it well enough. What I didn't understand was the "longer than he realizes."

TIMELINE
Feb 19, 2009 a week ahead of a visit by me to Jan
E-mail from Caron, Jan's mother

Jan will be confused by your appearance (you are actually here, who are you? you seem familiar) but she will have mixed emotions. Barry, I hope you won't be too disappointed . . . be prepared for a beautiful person, still happy and kind, but insecure and worried. Sit close to her, hold hands, and there will be lots to talk about. Her friends at the assisted living facility will be so happy for her that you finally came.

Did you know that they elected her as Queen of Valentines Day? There are pictures at the facility about this.
Bon Voyage!!
~Caron

18

"The way to love anything is to realize that it might be lost."
~C.K. Chesterton

The Last Goodbye?

We were in the living room of her small apartment at the assisted living facility. Around her were the things I hoped would help her memories. I looked at the pictures nailed on her "Jan Pink" walls, like the framed pictures of Paris where we traveled early in our marriage when we were as close to broke as we could get without actually being bankrupt. Was it that long ago that we cashed in our airline miles for a free ride to Paris? The hotel was all of thirty dollars a night, including breakfast. We became happy experts in restaurants with wonderful food at very low prices. Nearby was a painting of old Hawaii that I'd commissioned an artist in China to make for her. Did she even remember Hawaii?

The couch and chair in her apartment were overstuffed and cozy and splashed with some of her favorite fabrics that we'd brought from Tokyo to spread across the furniture. The bright golds and rich crimsons were always her favorite.

I sat in the chair. We had finished dinner. Outside, the late February sun was setting, making the room cozy and warm. She walked over to me and leaned down, focusing on my eyes. "Don't forget me."

Even now I can't tell if it was a plea that I keep her close. Or was she letting me go but asking that no matter where I went that I would bring our memories with me?

I once wrote about how Jan was so charming that she could get a fencepost to tell her its life story. But now I can't even ask her what she means because The Disease doesn't take questions, and she can no longer give answers.

She said it only once, looking at me. Her face showed no anger or sadness, or even love or affection. It was oddly blank, just her face, as if all her concentration was on getting those words correct and getting them out. Then she did something she rarely did anymore. She slid onto my lap. I put my arms around her and she relaxed against me, her head on my shoulder. For a while, there were no words.

I can cry now, as I write this. But I couldn't cry then. It would have upset her. And I didn't know . . . what did she mean? And how could she have this sudden moment of pure clarity? It was so important to her to tell me and had it been within my power, I would have given her anything.

If I just knew.

And then it got worse. She told me she wanted me to lie down in the bedroom, on the bed. At first, I thought she wanted me to rest, that she was worried about me because my day, which had begun in Tokyo when I got on the plane, was so long and was still going. So I went into the bedroom, fully dressed, and stretched out flat on the bed. She came in and stood on the other side of the bed and began taking off her clothes, and I wondered if she was getting ready to go to sleep. It was early, but she was now running on her own schedule. I waited, quiet, and as always, wondering and uncertain.

She didn't get into pajamas — odd, because she loves wearing red silk pajamas to bed. Instead, she kept undressing until she was naked and beautiful, soft and curved. Outside, the sun was gone and the room darkened.

She smoothed the covers and lay next to me, on my right side, and curled herself along my body. She had nothing on. Now I thought I knew what she needed, me to cuddle and hold her and stroke her and give her the comfort of our coming together, what we had shared so many times before in our love and our hunger to be close.

But I couldn't. I couldn't do this. I was afraid for me. It was the most selfish moment of my life, and it surprised me. If I gave her this now, I couldn't move on. This was the moment to decide. Is this what I must do to survive? To lie there, with clothes on, while she offers me her body . . . and not take it? There was no warning of this moment coming, no chance to discuss it with others. I had to decide and it had to be now.

She wanted to tell me why, but now the words are confused. It comes out like this: "I am flat and round. This is what I am."

I thought then that I knew what she meant; that she was there, naked and open to me as she has always been from our beginning. She says something else that is gibberish, but in my memory, this is what I heard: "This is my body. This is me. This is everything I have and I offer it all to you."

And I could not take it. Perhaps she wanted reassurance in our skin touching, perhaps there was some part of her that remembered our making love and she needed that. But I couldn't do this. Now, for the first time since our first kiss when my life began, I know I couldn't do this now or ever again.

In the twisted logic of The Disease, touching her, caressing her, would be somehow cruel of me. It is simply not allowed. She is defenseless and she needs care and protection. She is like a child, lonely and so often scared. And I am not her lover, I am her caretaker.

The first kiss was our first knowing that we were to be one. Now, in this darkened room, it was ending. Along the way there were a million kisses, a million nights of being together, or worse, being apart. It was never supposed to end at all, and now it ended like this.

I was still next to her for a while with no words. She got up and opened her closet and found her pajamas and put them on, first the top and then the bottoms. I got up and came around to her side of the bed to help her crawl in and pull up the covers and kiss her as I prepared to leave. Her eyes sought my face. Do you know who you are, I asked.

"My name is Jan."

"Do you know who I am, darling?"

She looked at me, as softly as she always had, but she couldn't answer. She had lost me.

TIMELINE
March, 2009 after my visit
E-mail from Caron, Jan's mother

Barry, I am so sad about the whole thing, but we have to be honest about where Jan is going, which is nowhere, and you still have lots of life left. I am hopeful that you will find a woman with whom you can share your life. It would be good for you, and couldn't possibly hurt Jan, who would never know or understand.

This progression from Jan to someone else in your life might take a few years, but nevertheless, it could happen, and I pray it does. I also hope that your taking care of her can continue, as we would all be lost without it.

19

"I have ever since (my wife's death) seemed to myself broken off
from mankind; a kind of solitary wanderer in the wild of life,
without any direction, or fixed point of view: a gloomy gazer on
the world to which I have little relation"
~Samuel Johnson

The Guilt of Love That May Someday Be

We have so many measures of time; hours, days, years.
Look at a clock and you can know, with certainty, where you are
in time with the rest of the world. It is exact.

With Jan, The Disease decided the timing of change, the
pace of her departure, and it will decide when she will reach the
final destination. So when people suggested that I consider
opening myself and my life to include someone else, there was
no timetable for how long I had been without Jan, and no
timetable for when I might begin again, if that was my decision.
It reminded me of the unspoken rule The Disease taught me:
When there is no rule, make one up as best you can.

Jan's mom, in her extraordinary e-mail, gave me permission
to choose what was next in my life, but with a thought that it
may be years before this happens. I had a similar, private
thought that I wanted to scream to the world: It has already been
years! And I don't even know how many.

A lot of people started their clocks on an "acceptable"
separation from Jan as May, 2008, when I placed her in the
assisted living facility and then returned alone to Asia to
complete my CBS News contract for covering Asia until it ended
in the fall of 2009. The May separation was clean, neat and there
was a clear physical break.

And it was wrong.

The intimacy was gone years before that benchmark, long
enough ago that I couldn't remember. And how many years had

it been since I lost Jan as a friend and wife and partner in a marriage, to be replaced by someone who needed me primarily as a caregiver?

When Diane suggested it was time to move Jan into assisted living, my first reaction was relief. Could the never-ending days of caregiving finally be over? Could the years of exhaustion and Sisyphus-like pushing against The Disease be finished, the struggle that would end in defeat no matter what I did? And so when these few close friends suggested that I find someone else, there was also an odd sense of relief, that there could be life with someone new. For so long, I hadn't considered life beyond what The Disease had stolen.

And then came a loud, insistent banging at the door and I opened it and in walked guilt. Guilt is a wide-ranging, hardworking thing. It twists decisions that we may instinctively know are right and makes them feel wrong. It hobbles our efforts at positive steps, and most days it puts in a few hours of overtime and stops us from taking those steps.

Guilt asked the key question: Was I a bad person for wanting love back in my life? It was not about sex. It was about no longer having a friend and partner and companion, no longer having someone to share the day with. Just thinking about it seemed a violation of what Jan and I had once been, a sin against our togetherness. After all, she couldn't help what was happening to her.

And in time, I realized that I couldn't help that I wanted a chance to love again. I didn't run out to find another woman. Instead, I ran out to find therapists to help me stop thinking or wanting this. There were psychologists, a hypnotherapist, and the psychiatrist, and phone calls to others who were on this same journey and could understand the guilt. And along the way I shared the tears and the terror that I felt I was a bad person because I was thinking about and wanting this.

And yet, their advice was remarkably similar. Leave the guilt behind. They suggested in their various ways that I had to decide this for myself, to focus on my own timing, and accept that my being alone had stretched across years even when Jan and I were together. And more than one warned me to brace myself for those who would not understand, those who would judge.

The professionals suggested that I try a new way of thinking; that this was not about Jan, it was about my life. I had not caused Jan's disease, I could not delay it, ease it, reverse it, stop it. They were wise, but this was not what I was asking of them. I wanted them to help me stop these thoughts about filling the emptiness with someone else. I found myself wandering into churches. I wasn't seeking God but absolution. A cleansing of my sin, because it seemed a sin, this wanting to be held again, wanting to feel the joy of holding someone I loved, wanting to bring pleasure by making someone else laugh.

Wanting to laugh.

For the first time since that night at Jan's apartment, that night I believed we would be together for the rest of our lives, I had to consider taking her out of my life equation and going it alone. Do I listen to my guilt, or to my gut? Whatever I did, there would be those who would accept and those who would accuse. I got a dose of this the hard way, a harsh rebuttal from one woman who stared at me and stated bluntly that I was "trolling for women."

I understand the sentiment. There were many who wanted an emotional death for me as slow and final and lonely as Jan's. For a time, I wanted the same fate. And yet, I did not think Jan would have accepted this from me. If loving her caused me to follow her into oblivion, it would have saddened her beyond measure. I can say, with faith, that she loved me more than that. And I, her. Had it been different, had I been the one with The Disease, I would never want her sucked into this darkness to remain there forever.

So fighting back took on a new resolve: I would not surrender to The Disease. Jan's life had always been about laughter and smiles, optimism and vibrancy, and about the sheer joy of living. This is the part of her that I now needed to honor. Friends saw this first, and in the seeing, they helped show me the way.

TIMELINE
March 30, 2009
E-mail from Amy Bickers, a long time friend

Dear Barry, I have wondered about this issue of you and relationships for a long time. You need love in your life. I think you should follow your heart. Jan will always be special to you and no one will ever replace her. But if she was sentient, she would want you to feel loved. You have my blessings and warm wishes and you should move forward.

There is simply nowhere else to go.

Hugs,
Amy

20

"We can live without religion and meditation, but we cannot survive without human affection."
~The Dalai Lama

21st Century Dating . . . Really?

I vacationed at our house in northern California for a while, a recess after one of my periodic visits with Jan in Seattle. This was becoming a good habit. I could see old friends for dinner by night, and by day sit and look out across the water and think.

Or perhaps better, not think. Just let the hours slide by. After a few days, I took a Sunday afternoon drive down the coast to San Francisco and stayed overnight with friends Kit and Russ Yarrow before catching the Monday afternoon flight to Tokyo. Wise friends.

We had dinner and then Russ called it a night, because he was up early the next morning facing a long commute to work. Kit and I sipped wine. I told her about how Jan was deteriorating, how hours after I left her I got an e-mail from a friend saying Jan was back to being angry because, Jan insisted, "she hadn't seen Barry in a year."

By now, I was growing accustomed to the changes and this one had been unfolding for a long time, so I could talk about it with Kit in a decidedly matter-of-fact way. I was a man alone, and this didn't meet with her approval. She brought her computer into the dining room. "Why don't you join an internet dating site?"

My initial reaction was to laugh out loud at her. Me? "Mr. Not A Good Catch?" I also thought internet dating sites were for adolescent techies and teens, or places where men went stalking women, the scary stuff of tabloids. I just assumed that someday I would meet someone; I just never quite focused on the "how." Besides, I had been married and out of circulation for twenty-five years and had no idea how people met these days.

When I met my first wife and again in 1984 when I met Jan, there were dates and dinners and slowly finding out about each other. In person. I get this method. But e-mail has replaced people chatting on a front porch, walking in a park, meeting for coffee, or over dinner.

Kit went to the website and signed me up. Whether it was because I'd had enough wine, or I'd had enough loneliness, I let her do it and watched with a fair dose of concern and, in all honesty, a bit of curiosity. We decided that my marital status was "separated." The form asked about one's "best physical attribute" and to my red-faced shame she answered "butt." I mumbled out an embarrassed thanks and as soon as I could, changed it to "hair" which I still have, thankfully.

What would people think? Did I dare mention that I had a wife with Alzheimer's Disease? And why wasn't I a good catch? I was well-traveled and had met people all over the world. Wasn't there some value in that?

A credit card number entered into the billing part of the website and, in that much time, I was now a member of the new generation of people who don't meet at churches, classes, or the office. You put yourself where anyone, everyone can see. Kit picked out the password: Phase2.

I didn't post a picture because I didn't want people from my office tittering over my meek efforts. And the profiles were screened to keep out information like an e-mail address that would reveal a person's identity.

I discovered that the dating site was very big on confidentiality and would send e-mails through its own system, sanitized, unless two people decided to trade information on their own. It was a safety feature of which I heartily approved. It would also let me look at profiles sorted by age, and I wanted any selections to be close to my age. There were a lot.

The process was oddly Victorian, a throwback to the era of writing letters one to another. It was learning about people by sending notes before you actually met, using the written word to best describe yourself and learn about their skills at describing who they were. The internet dating site itself, with its careful rules, was like a chaperone; there as long as you wanted it. And it was up to you to decide when or even if you cared to meet someone by phone or in person.

When I got back to Tokyo, I wrote my own profile and made strict rules for myself. If there was an initial contact, meaning if I wrote someone or they wrote me, and it was my turn for a response, the first thing I explained was that I was "separated" not by love's failure, but by Early Onset Alzheimer's Disease and that Jan was now in an assisted living facility.

For some, that was enough for a quick goodbye, if I got any response at all. For others, a matter of sympathy and the beginning of a discussion. As I further explained about Jan, some lost interest. It was too complicated and maybe, at the outset, I really didn't sound ready for this.

Yet, I didn't have the in-person chance to meet people because I was so far away and in very different cultures. If I was going to meet someone in San Francisco, Minneapolis, or Tokyo, it had better be someone interested in having dates that were about e-mails or long phone conversations.

I knew that many of my friends wanted me to try this because meeting people, no matter how it's done, can lead to finding that special one. But there was a loud nagging voice inside me. Could I allow anyone else in my life besides Jan? She would be here physically, for years to come. And I would always take care of her because I had loved what we had been to each other. But how hard do I hold on to what was? It was complicated. I was battered by questions from myself that I could not answer.

How long do we wait before we take the next step? There are no rules. I was making it up as I went along, and that was far more dangerous. I was guiding me. It was like the line about lawyers . . . a lawyer who represents himself has a fool for a client. Was I being a fool for giving myself permission to try this . . . for just myself?

It felt incredibly self-centered. I sat alone one night in the living room of the apartment in Tokyo, turned out the lights and closed my eyes and remembered how Jan had once been there, how she had chased away my loneliness when she first came into my life. Now, The Disease had taken her away, and her going made it more bittersweet for knowing what we once had.

I knew myself well enough to know what would happen if I stayed alone. I would dry up. I would cease to be. I wanted to love and be loved because that is how we feel alive as human beings, and it had been a long time since I felt alive. I had taken care of Jan as she diminished to the point that, mentally, she was almost a child. Now she was even less than that, and tomorrow she would be worse.

I decided. This was the moment to take a deep breath, sit up straight, brace myself for the anger of those who would not understand, draw strength from those who would. I felt like a diver standing on a cliff who feels terrified at how far down the water is, but vowing to make myself do this. I stepped off and plunged, with no idea what would happen when I hit the water.

It started with posting a profile. It was actually more frightening than diving off the cliff. There were responses that were lovely and understanding. There were responses that said I was not ready. There were responses so desperate that they scared me.

One was sweet but not hopeful from a woman in Denver:

Hi Barry,

Thank you for your lovely note. Japan would be the definitive long distance relationship! You sound like you have had an interesting life and have many stories to share. I'm so sorry about your wife's illness. How very difficult for you and your family. What a loss. Tell you what; if you find that you are going to be in Denver visiting your daughters, let me know and maybe we can share a glass of wine. I'm not ready for the challenges of the distance, but since you are a journalist and must enjoy writing, the worst case is maybe we could be pen pals!

Pen pals? I write all day long for a living and I didn't need more pen pals. However, Denver was a city I planned to visit often, as I answered:

I currently live in Asia but travel back to the US regularly, being drawn by family and a year-old granddaughter with a smile so bright you could land a 747 by it at midnight. Maybe I'm prejudiced?

Responses from others were more forthcoming, wanting to chat on the phone or meet when I was next in the United States. I went slowly and carefully, with all the confidence of a blind man walking through a minefield. There were a couple of lunches with women during visits to the US where I learned that photos and people don't always match. And there were phone calls — can they be called first dates? — sharing stories where you try to learn about someone from their voice and what they want to talk about.

There were people I met through the website in, of all places, Tokyo, including the ax-murderer woman. She wasn't the ax-murderer. She was worried that I might be. I discovered this on our first date over dinner. I had invited her to see my apartment, which was about a hundred yards from the restaurant. I later learned this was a big mistake on my part, but the offer came from ignorance and being somewhat rusty and nervous about all this. She said she couldn't come up because she didn't have my address and, therefore, hadn't left it with friends in case something happened to her.

Ah, I joked, as in what if I'm an ax-murderer and your friends wouldn't know where to look for the body, right? Some joke. That was exactly what she meant and so, chagrined, I walked with her for a while in the brightly-lit restaurant district and left her at the subway station. I walked home wondering what part of my well-traveled demeanor or Virginia gentleman charm made someone think I might be an ax-murderer.

In the end, I decided she was right in being self-protective and I apologized for being wrong, possibly pushy, and unforgivably ignorant. Before our next meeting, I sent her my address and phone number and invited her for dinner, which I cooked at the apartment. It was a lovely evening and I am glad to report that she survived with all limbs intact.

As for my cooking, it apparently didn't impress her because I never heard from her again. More proof that I was a bad catch, at least to some.

And all of it was part of learning.

It didn't stop there. One woman invited me to fly off to Madrid with her. We had talked — once — on the phone, and she had detailed the many affairs she'd had, which happened because she married her husband but never felt passion for him. I told her Madrid was a wonderful invitation and could I take it under advisement? Yikes.

I also kept up with that long-distance pen pal. I sent her a note that included this:

A benefit of this e-mail is that I can attach a picture of what I look like today . . . no more hair, teeth gone . . . the real me.

In return, there was this:

It's a great picture. You've got wonderful silver hair (it is yours, correct?) and I assume that when I saw your piece, that you also had teeth — you know TV and all . . .

And here I went again:

The hair is NOT SILVER. Good grief. It is . . . well . . . let's see, more like Danish, you know . . . really, really light blond, right? Platinum blond? White blond? Okay, maybe a touch silver, but just a touch. And I wonder to myself, when did that happen? Last week it was all brown and I was all young and now, silver hair. Let us hope that there is wisdom that comes with it.

Wisdom would be needed, for there was sadness in this person as she shared:

You asked, so here is my story . . . I was married at twenty-seven (old at that time) and my husband was twenty years my senior. He was always athletic (played pro football and semi-pro baseball), and when I bought him his first really good bicycle, he was smitten. He did seven rides across the country and was all set for a ride on the highest paved road in the world — sixteen-thousand feet in Peru. He was training on Mt. Evans, the highest paved road in North America — fourteen-thousand feet and right outside Denver, when he hit some really fine sand and gravel, going downhill on a road bike. The state had put an emergency call box right on the turn (rather than twenty feet away near the ranger station).

To make a long story short, he started to skid and hit the box. It tore his aorta and he died instantly. They never called me, but I knew something was wrong. I won't bore you with the rest of the story, but suffice it to say that I was happily married and still having fun. Another little detail is that we also worked together.

In one moment, I lost both my husband and business partner, and my life changed in ways I couldn't have imagined.

It seemed we were partners in loss. Hers was sudden.

With Alzheimer's, I explained, it is a slow drip of grief, and I was trying to fumble my way through life with that slow drip going on every day.

We traded phone numbers and started calling. Our e-mails and our sharing was a courtship, which I didn't realize at first. I felt myself opening up. As time went on, as we explored each others' lives and likes, we were two people growing closer. Now the questions were coming at me in a flood.

Was this right? Did I have something to offer, and was it a fair exchange because I was still married even if permanently and forever separated? I braced myself for a fresh round of accusations that I was abandoning Jan. No rules, no roadmaps, no guidelines except the raging conversations inside my head.

In time I made my way to Denver and we met for breakfast and then, a few days later, for a drink. It was at the lobby bar in the hotel where I was staying and we had our drink around 9 p.m. It was a quiet night and the barkeep was bored, so he closed the bar about 10 p.m. but let us stay. We managed a second glass of wine before he locked up.

We talked for five hours that night. And after I left town we called and talked by phone, sometimes for five or six hours or even more. There was something there that was making me feel alive again, and I was both excited and guilty, maybe in equal measure. What drove me toward her? I believed it was because she was strong and sensible and intuitive.

I wanted to be careful, and I needed to trust my own feelings. The trouble was that my feelings were having a raging debate. Part of me worried about how much I needed from someone, how wounded a bird I had become. Was it too much? Did I even know?

The other part argued that there was potential here, something special about this woman. In the end, my intuition and I came to an agreement . . . that maybe I could fall in love again and with her, and that meant I was ready for a new beginning.

Ready yes, but able?

Therein lies a tale.

TIMELINE
Winter, 2009
E-mail from a friend who was widowed from her first husband when she was in her 30s

Dear Barry,

Healing is finding peace with what is, while still cherishing all the rest. It will come, give it time. You never forget, you never stop loving and yearning, but there is still joy to be discovered. I was thinking about survivor guilt this morning on the way to work. Everyone I know who has been through the loss of a loved one suffers from guilt for something — some slight, a cross word, a promise broken, etc. But guilt is our way of believing we had the power to change the outcome if only we had . . . done something more, said something different.

We can't admit, at least for a long time, that we were powerless, utterly powerless in the face of the tsunami that hit us. For now, we are learning to be survivors, caretakers, the ones left standing.

21

*"All changes, even the most longed for, have their melancholy,
for what we leave behind is a part of ourselves. We must die to
one life before we can enter another."*
~Anatole France

Alone With My Soul at Midnight

It started happening when I would close my eyes and try to
sleep . . . a floating, queasy sensation of being in the air, adrift
with no firm place to stand, nothing to hold on to. And the
loneliness came with it, washing over me. It didn't really matter
where I was; in a hotel someplace in China, Indonesia on
assignment, or in the Tokyo apartment surrounded by familiar
things with the darkened city laid out below.

I tried to fend it off by drinking too many glasses of wine,
Scotch, or vodka before going to bed. Was there not an
anesthetic for my unquiet mind? Sometimes when sleep
wouldn't come and the feelings wouldn't ease, I would restlessly
turn on the bedside light and read a book, not because I cared,
but to distract from what came when the eyes were closed.
Words would blur on the page as the questions returned . . . was
it normal to want touching and being caressed? How many
million poems and plays have been written about this?

My contemplation was simpler and not very poetic. How
many more nights, I would wonder in the darkness, were left in
my life and would they all stretch for hours like this. Was it right
or wrong to want something different, someone in this bed with
me? Why weren't there any damn rules?

And there were other hauntings that came out when the
shadows ran deep. As Jan slowly slipped away, so did our
intimacy. There were reasons for this. She had faded until she no
longer seemed to feel the pleasure or have the interest in our
togetherness. So making love left me feeling not satisfied, but

selfish, that I was taking from her and she could not have as much back.

Second, there was my increasing sense of being a parent watching over her like a child. This can be numbing and repulsive to one's desires, no matter how much love is involved, or for me, the remembrance of what our love had once been.

What those around me didn't know was the effect this was having on me. It loosed the terrible part of every man that is his sexual insecurity. I discovered that I could not let go, could not release, could not have an orgasm when I was making love with her and we should be as one.

The wise advice is that you shouldn't hide things from those trying to help you, such as a friend or a therapist, a pastor or a priest. For the first time in my life, I ignored that. I was a man who could tell the entire world stories of other people's intense pain or joy but could not share with anyone this depth of my insecurity and the embarrassment of my own failing.

But at least when Jan and I still lived together and we were in bed at night and she was warm and next to me, I could listen to her soft breathing in sleep and I could drift back in time and memory. Across the silver screen of my midnight dreamings, I could replay how I had once thrilled and been thrilled by her. Memories are rich and good, but they cannot nourish forever. A silver screen can flicker and the moving pictures of the mind can dim.

By the time I placed Jan in the Alzheimer's facility we had not, as they would put it in a gentler era, lived as man and wife for so long that I couldn't recall with any accuracy how long it had been. Certainly a few years. Now that she was gone and I was alone at night, my mind would taunt me: You have lost everything, including that which makes you a man.

There were answers to the sleepless, endless, dark shadowed nights. One was to accept and live as I was and endure these nights forever. The other was to give life another try, and that was why I reached out to see if there might be someone else.

And now that I thought I had found just such a lovely person, it was time to decide if I dared or even could reach for just a little more. These are the things I debated and rolled about in my conscious mind. What I didn't realize was that there was a hidden danger building inside me, that the years of dealing with Jan had created a huge reservoir of traumas that would demand attention or else would never heal.

I had gone through years where each day began as a question mark, and each night was either relief that Jan was stable or sadness that I had spotted some new decline. Watching her falter, like the days when the unreasoned anger would seize her, fed the trauma of knowing I had lost that much more of her and of us. Then there were the intense, searing traumatic moments . . . saying goodbye and getting into a car and leaving her behind in an assisted living facility, flying back to Asia alone and realizing that we would never be together again, being in an empty apartment that she once gaily filled and that she would never even see again.

There is a theory of trauma therapy suggesting that we humans store traumatizing events in our bodies, while other animals can release it immediately. An animal that has escaped sudden death literally gets up and shakes it off, rejoins the herd and goes on about its life basically and instinctively back to normal. The trauma is gone and, with it, the fear. Humans, because most of us have not been trained in how to let it go, will store the trauma inside. It may take a new or different event, sometimes years later, to release it.

You might or might not believe the theory. Some don't. I do. And with reason. It unfolded all at once; the sadness inside, the terror of no longer being a real man, the trauma of loss, the wondering if there was enough left of me as a person to persuade someone new that we could create something together.

In the many phone calls and e-mails with this someone new, there was a potential relationship building. She and I had shared similar emotions about loss . . . her husband to accidental sudden death, Jan to a wasting disease. It brought us together first as friends. She offered gentle guidance on surviving and rebuilding drawn from the ashes of her own grief.

And there were other things we developed that must seem silly to some. For me, one was the long forgotten pleasure of calling and sharing the events of the day with someone else, each of us talking about work or what had happened in the world. I hungered for conversations so normal, and for the celebration of ordinary life.

In time, we wondered if there could be more. And all this time, hiding unspoken in the background, my doubt that even if given the chance, was there was still a man, a lover, inside of me. And in more time, with passing months, with hesitation and trepidation and a thousand more telephone hours discussing the consequences and the pleasures, wondering who would congratulate us and who would condemn us, there was finally a day when oceans and continents were crossed and we were together. And with it, almost naturally, returned what I once feared was lost to me . . . the intensity of intimacy.

In that moment and then the sweet afterward, in the holding tight and the catching of breath, there was relief giving way to the sheer wonder of what had happened. Did this mean that there was, now, a chance for a different future? Could I have this woman in my life and would she have me? What extraordinary possibilities seemed there, just right there in that moment, for the dreaming and the reaching and the taking.

And then in stalked The Disease. It struck when she was folded into my arms. It came, as so often, with brutality and without warning. It happened within seconds. My body began vibrating, from head to toe. Let me be clear—not shake or convulse, but a steady trembling or vibration. She and I had talked before about how trauma escapes out of the body and one rule is, don't try to stop it. If you interrupt it, experts say, the trauma release goes back to zero, and it starts again.

She held me tenderly, but very carefully. "Do you feel that, sweetie?" she asked in just barely a whisper, masking what was clearly her growing alarm.

"Yes." I was as alarmed as she was since I had never felt my body tremble like this before. Tinged with the fear was embarrassment, that at this of all moments, I would have some kind of reaction that I couldn't understand and could not explain.

There was a moment of pause, of her holding my trembling body, of letting the trauma find its way out. "Do you know why you are trembling?"

I had no answer, but I wanted one, as my body rocked against her and I could not stop it. As I searched for some explanation, I began thinking about how I had tried caring for Jan to protect her from The Disease, had helped Jan cover up the effects and had pretended with Jan for years that nothing was different. At times she believed it. And at times, so did I.

And as I thought, I began weeping. Not just crying but weeping so hard it was difficult to breathe so that I could weep even more. It left me choking for air. I covered my face with my hands. I pressed harder against this bewildered and scared woman who now held me, trying to offer comfort in her softness and her warmth.

My body was both trembling from the trauma and shaking back and forth from my tears, and I was struggling, trying to make words through this. "I was supposed to protect" . . . sobbing so I could not talk for a moment, then trying to get a breath . . . "protect her and I didn't" . . . then unable to talk as more tears poured out. "It was my job, my one job . . . to care for her and to protect her."

The same words kept pouring out of me . . . love meant protecting Jan and she trusted me, but for all my love, I had failed her. Because of that, in my mind, I had failed as a man and a husband. It would be good to make up elegant phrases with more depth or meaning, but in the midst of trembling and tears, all I could do was say it over and over . . . and over. I was a man, a man's job is taking care of those he loves, and I had failed. And look what my failure had done to Jan.

And quietly and generously, this woman who thought as I did, that we had a chance at our own love, gently shared what should have been our moment with Jan. Trying to ease my agony, she told me that I had done nothing wrong, that I had made no mistakes that made Jan's disease worse, that I did not cause it.

Words. Sometimes they mean everything, sometimes nothing. Her words, so sweet and reassuring, could not at first penetrate. In time, I calmed down. I rolled over and found tissues and blew my nose and rolled back to hide in her arms and her tenderness . . . and it started all over again. I could not . . . damn it! . . . could not stop. The weeping overwhelmed, the tears poured, and I was shaking again. And then, I would gain control. And then, lose it.

When we envision scenes of the wonder of coming together as two people discovering their chance at love, we have visions of fireworks and, if we are well trained by Hollywood, we hear the swell of an orchestra. We do not see the man suddenly dissolve into trembling and tears.

But so it was. This was release from years of not having been a lover, and of trauma stored in my body that was letting go. And there was also a desperate effort trying to let go of the guilt . . . my merciless unforgiving guilt . . . for failing Jan.

We often tell ourselves that it is better to let it out. Well, this was letting it out; this was release but with torment. It was not relief, it was agony.

In time I finally quieted, and we talked as she held me. I put my emotions into words, and that helped. We talked of my guilt and how, in my mind, I needed to somehow come to believe that I had done nothing wrong in my caring for Jan, that The Disease could not have been stopped.

It was good making it into words, but it did not erase the emotions and the feelings of guilt. That is not so easy. Parts of it still remain inside. More will come out in time, and at a time probably not of my choosing. I call Alzheimer's The Disease. I capitalize the letters because, to me, it is a viable and known enemy. In my mind I give it face and form. And one way to beat The Disease is to keep going when The Disease is taking Jan down and stretching it tentacles trying to drown me as well.

The Disease and I both know this. It is the arena of our personal war.

TIMELINE
April, 2009
E-mail from Jim, whose wife also suffers Early
Onset Alzheimer's

My current situation is not unlike yours in that I have met someone fairly recently and have had to work through the problems of being a person of uncertain status. I imagine we could spend a long time discussing the unique position of loving one's wife while loving another person as well.

Look forward to talking with you.

~Jim

22

"The real voyage of discovery consists not in seeking new landscapes, but in having new eyes."
~Marcel Proust

Persons of Uncertain Status

We are nervous at our first meeting, sitting in a booth in one of those upscale chain restaurants that dot American cities. Outside it is well over ninety degrees. Inside the air-conditioned air has a dry chill to it. Around us the waiters flitter as they are trained to do, offering refills or asking if everything is okay.

It is a normal place on a weekday afternoon. But we are not normal. In this little booth there exists a private universe unknowable to many of our friends and even family. I look at this other couple and see a mirror I cannot find anywhere else. That is why I have flown across the country to sit in this booth and see if there is another human being on this path who understands.

The admission fee to our tiny universe is costly. To sit in this restaurant booth, you must bring doubt, guilt, a search for moral clarity without clear guidelines and most of all . . . a spouse with Early Onset Alzheimer's Disease who is now in a care facility.

There is one more price of admission; having someone new in your life that you now love in a world where some will call you an adulterer who has broken his wedding vows, and paint her with a Scarlet A.

And that woman must have the self-confidence to face the accusations of being "That Woman" that some will say lured you from a sick wife, stole you away from your role as caregiver, found you at your emotionally most vulnerable and marched in to plant her flag. "That Woman," the accusers will say with fingers pointed at her, "is a heartless gold digger."

There are ground rules for our meeting. They cannot be identified using either of their real names or the city where they live. I will call them Teresa and Jim. They are nationally known and accomplished in their respective fields, she as a writer and college professor and he as a health care professional specializing in geriatrics.

They ask for anonymity because there are those in their professional lives and within their circle of friends who will not see redemption in their love, but the violations of sacred marriage vows.

Weren't those vows clear enough when we stood at the altar and pledged . . . 'till death do us part?

"But," Jim asks, leaning forward a bit. "When is the death of a marriage?"

This will be a central topic during our time together, and tied to it, is the question of how Jim and I define ourselves. We don't fit any category—we don't feel married, widowed, or single. Some may call us separated, but we are not that either, nor are we divorced.

Jim labels us this way: "You and I are persons of uncertain status."

And that leads to critical questions that neither of us ever dreamed would define our lives, but now must be debated and answered with thought and care.

First: Are we still in a marriage?

Second: Have we broken our wedding vows by falling in love with another woman?

"Society is becoming more accepting that the definition of a marriage is a relationship," Jim says.

He points out that more and more states now accept as law that two people of the same sex can be married. It makes marriage not about gender, but about the existence of a conscious relationship between two people. And when the consciousness is lost on one side, usually through death, the relationship ceases to be.

Except that with Alzheimer's the consciousness dies inside the brain while the body lives on for some unknown period of years. Like Jim's wife, Jan is still alive. Jan still gets her hair cut or her nails manicured as long as someone walks her through the process. She still loves Barry, although she no longer recognizes that I am that person when I am with her. Her Barry lives in photographs of a younger us, or long-ago memories.

Jan lives alone in a world that I cannot know or penetrate, and can only guess how or if I even affect it. She is gone to me.

Jim asks, "Is that still a marriage?"

He brings up an idea that he calls drama. It is what we craft in our minds about our own lives, how we plot our personal days and destinies and what Shakespeare meant when he wrote: *"All the world's a stage, and all the men and women merely players . . . they have their exits and their entrances. And one man in his time plays many parts."*

It's what makes someone a functioning person, says Jim, a person who can make decisions and choices and then respond and react.

Plotting our lives with our own decision making is as basic as deciding what to cook for breakfast, how to handle a meeting at the office, a coaching problem at Little League, deciding whether to make a U-turn or go around the block.

"And when called upon to do something they cannot do," Jim says of people, "they will do what they can." He pauses to emphasize this next key thought: *"If* they can do anything at all."

This is the axis on which our morality now turns, as defined not by us but by The Disease. Because of Alzheimer's Disease our wives can no longer maintain their half of the conscious relationship that is critical for what we call a marriage.

"So," he asks, "can you have a marriage without a relationship?"

As I sip coffee, Teresa interrupts my thoughts with one more vital piece of the jigsaw. "You are not the ones who left the relationship," she reminds Jim and me. "Your wives left you."

Teresa reminds us of this story:

(CBS/AP) The husband of retired Supreme Court Justice Sandra Day O'Connor has struck up a romance with a woman who is a fellow Alzheimer's patient and lives at the same assisted living center, according to a television news report. The retired justice isn't jealous about the relationship and is pleased that her husband is comfortable at the center, the couple's son, Scott

O'Connor, told KPNX in Phoenix in a broadcast that aired Thursday. "Mom was thrilled that Dad was relaxed and happy," Scott O'Connor said.

John O'Connor was diagnosed with Alzheimer's 17 years ago and was sad when he moved into the assisted living center, his son said. "Forty-eight hours after moving into that new cottage he was a teenager in love," Scott O'Connor said. "He was happy."

(http://www.cbsnews.com/stories/2007/11/13/national/main3494 982.shtml)

The world generally praised the amazing love of Mrs. O'Connor accepting that her ill husband, lost in Alzheimer's Disease, can find some form of happiness with another woman.

"But," asks Teresa, "what if it had been the reverse and it was Sandra Day O'Connor who found a new love while her husband is suffering from Alzheimer's? The reverse would not have been okay to many people."

Jim and I are struggling to write a code of conduct that helps us honor what we have now found . . . love, companionship, a renewed sensual worth, laughter and excitement in learning about someone new that we love as we leave behind the tears.

Jim put it like this, "We want to claim and create our own realities."

Because The Disease takes, demands, and steals, we can no longer live in the world most people inhabit because their morality is not our reality.

That is the key reason why Teresa wants anonymity. Those who encouraged her to go find happiness may turn on her for finding that happiness with a "married" man. She tells us how she didn't want to become involved with a man who had been divorced. "I had found that usually the divorced men I encountered were the ones who were at fault in the break-up of their marriages, and they hadn't learned from it. Or they were often, to use the cliché, emotionally unavailable because of their anger at their ex-wives."

She and Jim met because they were members of the same internet dating site. "Initially, when Jim contacted me and said that he was separated, I rebuffed him and wrote him back to contact me if or when his situation changed, thinking that he was the classic adulterer looking for an affair. It was only after he wrote back with a more detailed explanation of the circumstances of his involuntary separation that I was willing to meet him, although I still had many qualms about the situation."

They were both nervous and a little dubious at their first meeting. Jim remembers looking at her and thinking, "Well, it's only an hour out of my life." And then they started talking, and the first meeting turned into hours of conversation that led to seeing each other again and again. Teresa found in Jim's character a key reason that she could trust him and wanted to make her life with this particular man.

"Here is a man who cared for his wife even when it was dangerous to his own health," she says. "This is a man who can give everything because he loves a woman. It shows how deeply he can love. We should celebrate these men, not condemn them because their wives left them and they found someone else."

What she says is true. Jim and I cared for our wives out of love. When the person we loved went away from us, not in a day or a week, but over years, we never dreamed we would find that kind of love again.

Jim shared his years of being the main caregiver for his wife, and I nod my head knowingly. We brought all the love and comfort that we knew how to give, even to the point of threatening our own health. We adjusted our finances and watched salaries and savings diminish, and yet that and more would have been an acceptable sacrifice if it had made a difference. Did it matter that we knew how futile these efforts would be? It didn't stop Jim from trying, and it didn't stop me from despair when The Disease gained new ground.

We talk about those who believe they have the right to judge us. Jim introduced two concepts that let me consider the place and importance of various people, and use that to weigh their influence. Jim labels these as status and eligibility. The woman who is now in my life has high status because she has a stake in making it work for us.

As for a friend of Jan's who might disagree with my treatment choices? She can feel as she does and tell me what she thinks, but her status in my life is significantly lower.

Jim brings in the second idea: eligibility, as a way to set status. Put simply—there are people who have the right, by experience or knowledge, to help guide us. "Someone who has walked in your shoes has eligibility," he says. "Or an expert in Alzheimer's Disease is eligible because he or she has experience and specific knowledge that we don't. In a baseball game, there are players and fans and sportscasters who watch each play and can offer their opinions. But only the umpire has the right to call balls and strikes, safe or out, so he is the only one eligible to make those decisions."

In a baseball game, it is pretty clear who is in charge. In our lives, in our situation, Jim and I must decide for ourselves who is eligible. It really isn't that difficult. It took time for me to hear what those with medical experience were telling me, and once I began to listen—Jim would say that was giving their advice and information high status because of their eligibility—I was surprised at how often they agreed among themselves on what was best for Jan and for me.

And then there were others trying to influence me and demanding high status by the force of their anger or the strength of their own opinions. For a while, I listened and reacted to them not because they were experts on either Alzheimer's, or caregiving, or even on Jan's life at that point, but because they were loud.

Jim faced much the same. "They are performing a degradation ceremony. They are kicking us out of the community of what they consider respectable people because we violated their standards. We must say back to them, you are not eligible to do this to us because you don't have the competence to make that call, you don't have relevant experiences."

They are not the umpire unless, because of guilt, we allow them that role.

"Survivor guilt," clarifies Teresa.

As I nod my head in agreement, Jim asks me a practical question. "Where does that guilt take you?"

I flounder to answer. It has driven a whole series of decisions about caring for Jan that are, in fact, more about my guilt for not being the sick one, for having the life that is blossoming and not the life that is shutting down.

I tell them how I hired a companion who would visit Jan three or four times a week in the care facility. The companion reports in her e-mails that their outings are cheerful and upbeat. In truth, Jan did not remember these outings a minute or an hour later. And is Jan "happy" in the moments with the companion? It is another question that no one can answer. What she says, when she can make sentences we understand, changes day to day. And the concept of "happy" is now beyond her words.

I ask Jim about e-mails I get from those who visit Jan, telling me she is "upbeat" or "today she was engaged." This, despite the fact that Jan's language and memory are failing, and she shows other serious signs of ongoing deterioration.

Some people, explains Jim, will fill in the blanks from their own need to have the old Jan there. "A friend might say to her, 'Jan, isn't it fun getting our hair cut?' and Jan nods her head and says 'YES!' and it seems like she is engaged. They have not pressed their nose against the reality."

"I can't really blame them," I respond. "God knows I didn't want to press my nose against reality, either."

It is funny that when I first met them, they sat stiffly and properly through afternoon coffee and then dinner and hours of conversation. Yet the next day, at breakfast, they trusted me enough to allow themselves to touch each other, or hold hands, or affectionately rub each other's arms in front of me.

We do not say this next part out loud because it does not need saying in our peculiar little universe. There is a line. On one side is the past. Those were the years spent fighting The Disease, and the endless dark nights when we slept next to the woman we cared for and loved. And in that darkness we choked back tears because the woman The Disease left behind wouldn't understand why we cry, and the crying would only scare her.

On the other side of that line is the chance at a new love and caring and experiences with someone else. Not everyone will choose to cross that line. When Jan started leaving me, I didn't want anyone else. Then, as time went on and I started reaching out to see if there might be someone, it painfully drove home what I had lost. These were not women I wanted to be with the rest of my life. There were several I didn't want to be with the rest of the evening.

It is Teresa who asks the question Jim and I cannot answer. We can only hope that we have guessed right. "If you really love someone, would you want them to be alone because you went away from them?"

Would Jan? Would Jim's wife?

The answer Jim and I have found may only work in this private little universe, but that is where Jim and I shall live for the rest of our lives.

TIMELINE
June, 2009
Note from Pat Ness, who helped me find the assisted living facility

With the physical death of a loved one, we can openly mourn our loss at a funeral or memorial service. But there is no such ritual to support us in an Alzheimer's loss.

Alzheimer's disease is called "AMBIGUOUS LOSS" (from the book by the same name, written by Pauline Boss). Our loved one is no longer capable of participating in our lives; in our marital relationship, in parenting our children, in making the many decisions we used to share.

When my mom suffered from Alzheimer's and no longer recognized me as her daughter, I remember walking down the street and being angry at strangers, saying to myself, "How can you go on with your lives at a time when I'm experiencing such sorrow?"

And when my mother would stare at me blankly not knowing who I was, I wanted to shake her and say, "Snap out of it! Be my mom again!"

But Mom was not there. Or was she?

~Pat

23

*"You can clutch the past so tightly to your chest that it leaves
your arms too full to embrace the present."*
~Jan Glidewell, author and newspaper columnist

The War Within

I had a friend, a producer at *CBS News Sunday Morning* who
had traveled to the Soviet Union and worked on stories with me.
Together we did a profile on Rudolf Nureyev coming back to
dance at the Kirov in what was then known as Leningrad,
renamed St. Petersburg. It was Nureyev's first return to the
Soviet Union since he defected in 1961. A few years later my
friend developed cancer and struggled with chemotherapy.
When he went into the hospital, the cancer ate at him, shrinking
him, changing him.

When I asked to come visit him, he said no. My guess was
that he did not want my last memory of him to be as a shriveled
sick man, helpless and ill on his deathbed. Better to remember
him as he once was; full of energy and enthusiasm, loving his
work. I think about this because I reached a point of wondering
how long I could absorb Jan's changes, and how much more I
could stand as I saw myself erased out of her life.

Each new visit was about seeing how much she had lost,
such as her ability to find a word or make a sentence. And there
was pain in seeing her stare hard at me, this woman I love, who
now couldn't place me. There would be a flicker, a moment
where I thought she saw something, and then it was gone.

And even so, I'm not sure those moments were real. How
could I know? She cannot tell me. She doesn't understand,
because she is in a world apart from the rest of us, a different
world even from the others around her with their Alzheimer's.

She still talks about someone called "Barry." He is a part of
her daily life and as best I or anyone else can tell, they still have

conversations. One day when the dentist came to the assisted living facility, she went cheerfully for a routine exam because, as she later explained, "Barry told me to do it." In fact, I had told her no such thing.

That Barry, the one alive somewhere in her memory, is the one she still hears. She takes comfort in their togetherness. I have no influence on what he says or what he tells her. On one visit when I went to see her, we went to dinner at her brother's house. It was just the four of us, chatting about the remodeling they were doing and how it was going.

I thought Jan would feel comfortable, this was her brother and his wife, after all. Jan was having a good time. Later her mother shared the rest of the story. As Dave and I were talking, Jan and Marie were in the kitchen and Jan turned to Marie and said, "Who is that man out there? He's really cute, isn't he?"

"That man" was me. How nice it was, Jan's mom said, that even if Jan didn't know who I was sitting at a table a few feet away, she was still attracted to me. To me, it raised one of those questions I had been putting off. Did I want to see her someday when she had deteriorated to the point where she could no longer feed herself or use a toilet, take a shower, or dress? And how about when she could no longer walk by herself, when her body slips into the end stage—the vegetative state? It is coming, it is out there. The Disease fully intends to make it so.

I discussed this with Rob Blinn, the therapist who helped me with PTSD. He put my ongoing visits watching Jan change into one sentence, "It's like you are going to the same funeral, over and over again."

How many times could I experience fresh grief? And I also needed to accept that no future modern medical miracle will bring back from the dead the brain cells killed off by The Disease. Which means what is forgotten is truly gone. And that included me.

"If you see her once a week or once a year," counseled Jullie Gray, our care manager, "it won't make a difference to Jan, because she won't remember."

I wondered how Jan would feel. Is this how she wants to be remembered? Is this how she wants us to end? It was like my friend with the cancer; when is the point where we stop wanting those we love to see us as we falter and fade. Would she be horrified at what is ahead? Would she prefer that I let her go, let her die if a moment provides the opportunity, before she reached that stage?

I don't know because I didn't ask her. It took Jan being hurried to the hospital from the assisted living facility to force me into wondering about how and when Jan's life should end. As her husband, I am the decision maker (this varies from state to state), and I don't know her wishes.

The medical incident started when Jan developed abdominal pain and our care manager, Jullie Gray, sensed something serious and quickly drove her to the emergency room. They diagnosed diverticulitis, an inflammation of what looks like tiny pouches in the lining of the colon. The result can be a dangerous infection spreading throughout the body. The treatment options range from antibiotics (with fingers crossed) to emergency surgery.

For a normal person, this would be tough. You cannot eat because the colon must not be agitated. This gives the inflammation a chance to heal on its own while the antibiotics fight off any infections caused by leakage. During this time, the body gets fed and medicated by intravenous (IV) tubes. It is about being in a strange place in a strange bed with nurses and doctors poking and prying day and sometimes night.

For Jan, as the uncomprehending patient, it was a horror movie that stretched endlessly day into night, leaving her in a state of fearful, terrified disorientation, instinctively seeking escape from the hospital. The first problem came with the IV drips. She could not understand what they were for, so she yanked them out. Then she couldn't accept being confined to bed. She wanted to walk around like she did at the facility, so she would just get up and go, leaving the IVs behind.

Dealing with the nurses ignited her anger and, at one point, she struck out at a nurse. She could not understand where she was, or why, and was instead reacting in raw fear. By day, there were family visitors and Jody, the woman I had hired some months earlier as Jan's occasional companion. They stayed with her, walking with her in the hallway. It was not always sedate. At one point Jody found herself pulling Jan away from an elevator door. It was a wrestling match. Jan was leaving "right now," and only Jody's physical force stopped her.

By night, the hospital arranged for a sitter in the room who would watch over Jan, help her navigate to the bathroom, keep her from pulling out the IV drips. The nurses were dubious about giving Jan the anti-anxiety medication we were already using at the assisted living facility. They soon came around.

The hospital stay—I called it the hospital siege—went on for three days until the antibiotics worked, the problem eased, and surgery was no longer on the table. For the moment. Jullie Gray took Jan back to the assisted living facility just before lunch and watched as Jan found her way to her seat at her table in the dining room. Someone asked where she had been and Jan answered cheerfully, "I was on a boat trip." And calm returned.

But it was the beginning of a new turmoil. The surgeon wanted a colonoscopy to see if he still needed to operate and remove part of the intestine. Preparation for a colonoscopy means the bowels must be flushed beginning the day before the procedure. The patient cannot eat any meals the day before, nor breakfast the morning of the procedure. Back and forth we went with ideas and plans and strategies until we realized there was no way we could put Jan through this.

Since she could not comprehend why the procedure was needed, she would simply fight whoever tried making her do this, maybe fighting back literally. Her existence was about maintaining her routine, which meant dinner at night and up in the morning at her regular time for breakfast and lunch.

Which is why Caron, seeing this more clearly than I, sat down one day during the colonoscopy debate and sent me an e-mail that asked the questions I had not faced in my narrow focus on the need for the colonoscopy.

"I must ask you; do you think this procedure is necessary? What exactly is it for? Jan has maybe two years more in which we can enjoy her, and she can respond to us. Is it to prolong Jan's life? If so, why?"

Why? Well, because that is what we as a society instinctively do. I had signed orders that Jan be resuscitated in the event of an emergency, and I did so without hesitation, and worse, without thought. To me it was automatic because that is how we care for someone we love. But is it?

How I wish Jan and I had talked. It would have been easy for us to write our desires down when she could still do that, shortly after the diagnosis. How many times in my imagination can I hear myself just saying it; "Darling, let's write an essay that spells out what kind of care we want as we approach the end of life." But I never said it out loud. Because it meant putting the inevitable into words, and that would mean admitting the end of hope.

In asking people about their desires, the answers are surprisingly similar: Don't keep me alive (the person will say) if my life is about tubes and machines and I am not even conscious. And if it seems just that simple . . . it isn't.

I talked on the phone at some length with Dr. Margaret Faut Callahan, Dean of College of Nursing, at Marquette University in Milwaukee, WI. "My mother had Alzheimer's Disease" she told me. Dr. Callahan's research interests are in the areas of pain management, health policy, and palliative/end-of-life care. "Mother had not communicated with us for two and a half years. Near the end she had not eaten or been able to drink anything for two to three weeks, and had not urinated for well over a week. This was really end of life."

Dr. Callahan and her sister stood at the bedside with her mother. "My sister started singing 'When Irish Eyes Are Smiling.' I looked down at my mother and saw a tear rolling down her cheek. We took it as a sign from God telling us that she will be okay."

We cannot always know, she said, what is happening in the brain near the end of life, or how much awareness our loved one has. And this can be a difficult moment. Do you yell for nurses and start inserting tubes, or do you look down on your loved one and say that he or she would not want to endure a few more moments or days of technology-sustained existence.

Dr. Callahan pushed the question a step further. If her mother was able to hear a song and respond even in a comatose state, could she also suffer pain from any treatment but not be able to tell anyone?

Within her story there is a plea from someone who is both expertly trained, as well as sadly and personally experienced; do not wait to have the end of life discussion when the family is gathered at a hospital bedside, often due to an emergency or sometimes without warning.

"People who deal with end of life when they are thirty-year-olds," she said, "always do it better because they don't think they are dying."

And Alzheimer's has its own special torment, that for some, even near the end, the body still looks normal even though it is as decimated as a disease like cancer or AIDS would leave it. It makes acceptance of the illness difficult.

Bonnie Dank, the sister of my old friend, is the Psychiatric Nurse Practitioner at Copper Ridge, a 126-bed facility in Maryland with outpatient care for the "Memory Impaired." It is affiliated with Johns Hopkins Medical Center and part of the Episcopal Ministry for the Aging.

She also trained as a pastoral counselor, more a hospital-based spiritual counselor than a member of any clergy. And she uses that training almost every day dealing with the spiritual part of the individual. She shared a story with me, of Alzheimer's acceptance, hard and sad but final.

"I remember showing some pictures of an MRI (magnetic resonance imaging) brain scan to a woman whose mother was in the terminal phase of Alzheimer's. The woman still kept thinking that her mother would wake up and talk to her, recognize her. I had spent weeks trying to explain that that was not going to happen.

"Finally, I showed her the pictures and said, 'She doesn't have any brain left.' It was shocking. But the woman finally realized that her mother was gone and would exist only in her memory. She was then ready to stop all the futile treatments and let go of this body in the bed with her mother's name on it."

Drawing on her own daily experiences that often means talking with families, Bonnie asked the questions of me that she so often asks of others.

"How much of her, the Jan that you married, is still there? If she could not appreciate the richness of colors or laugh at the memory of giving away the Hopper book, or appreciate how she became an anchor on the news, would she still find her life worth living? There is a time when families have to recognize that the physical body is no longer the person they knew and loved and move on. You don't stop loving, you just do it in a different way so as not to hurt or scare this stranger. You do this so that you can remember the beauty that was before. That is the memory you want to keep with you."

TIMELINE
June, 2009
E-mail from Annie Marshall, Jan's friend from their Seattle TV news days

Try not to feel guilty. Jan did tell me when we had lunch here in October, 2007, that men need someone to take care of them and that she wants someone to take care of you. To be honest, when Jan sent me the e-mail telling me about her diagnosis, the thought that shot into my mind like an arrow was that she would commit suicide if she still could, because she would not want to put you or anyone else through the agony.
~Annie

24

"Live as if you were to die tomorrow. Learn as if you were to live forever."
~Mahatma Gandhi

Finally . . .

Someone once said of great art that we do not own it, we merely take care of it for our lifetime and then it is passed on to the next caretaker. When I fell in love with Jan, I thought it would be forever, but I was wrong. I merely had her for that time when she was passing through, touching lives, caring for others, and making me her life.

Jan had a belief that we create our own happiness. When you wake up and face a day feeling that way, the days can be good. Hers were. And because of her, so were many of mine.

In early 1994, while living in London, she set her sights on taking all of us on a safari in Kenya. It was crazy expensive, so we shifted dates to the week after the Christmas holidays to get a better rate and worked with Emily to adjust her school schedule in the States. This was a year in the planning. Julie was living with us while doing a semester at an acting academy.

Jan was the driving force behind the idea. She worried that Kenya had a rocky political future and we needed to go now, before it became dangerous—and she was right because that's exactly what happened a few years later. She felt quite strongly that the girls should see the African wildlife and a beautiful part of the world they had never experienced.

That was Jan's mantra; don't give the girls presents, give them experiences. She did the planning. My job was to pay for it, and this I would cheerfully do. She was using a London travel agency, arranging an itinerary and debating where we would go and how we would get there and the various cost options.

And then came Rwanda in 1994, and I was sent to cover the aftermath of that country's self-inflicted genocide that led Hutus to machete rival Tutsis into pieces, even those hiding in rural churches where they sought sanctuary. The tide then turned. The Hutus were driven into neighboring Zaire (now called the Democratic Republic of Congo), and they fled by the tens of thousands, exhausted, to a bleak volcanic plain.

There was no sanitation, no water, and no way to stop deadly cholera and dysentery once the epidemics got started. It was, without doubt, the worst story I had covered to that point in my career. To me, this was Africa for those few weeks; dust, heat, and death. And the next morning, it started all over again.

There were so many bodies stacked up every day that bulldozers scraped out trenches for shallow mass graves. And still more died. I called Jan daily and talked with her about normal stuff, and that kept me balanced. But one day, she had an agenda when I called. The travel agent needed to know about our safari now, even though it was about three months away. Say yes, or cancel.

I sat in the dusty, tented camp area at the airport where journalists had set up, hunched over and talking with her on the satellite phone. Come back to Africa, where I was now surrounded by the dead and the soon to be dead? In my emotional state, the idea was simply insane, unthinkable. Don't you hear me? I wanted out of here, not talk of coming back. Out!

But she would not accept that. She knew the safari was an experience that would be an amazing gift we could give each other and a stunning adventure for her stepdaughters.

But really, do I have to have this conversation now? Can't they wait?

No. She would not be put off. Answer now.

Perhaps it was some instinct that drove her on that call. She knew the Rwanda story because she had gone to the London Bureau and watched our pieces coming through on the satellite headed for New York and the CBS Evening News. She saw my report on the babies dying at the orphanage and she knew from the tone of my voice that it had shredded my heart. Why the innocent, why always the innocent who suffer? This was the stuff of nightmares, and there were those as well, if and when I actually slept. But she had some instinct, some persistence that I didn't comprehend at first.

I paused and held the phone and looked around where people were dying a few yards away for lack of a gallon of water and some salt. Life in that place, at that moment, was that fragile and that easily gone. And then I got it—what she believed and had always told me. If life is fragile, then do your best to love what you have, in that moment, at that time. This was not about a vacation or travel plans or any of that. This was Jan knowing that Barry needed to see past this horror and opt for the future, for life and for love of his children and family, and not surrender to the horror in front of him.

I told her yes, book the safari. And forever after that I remembered her lesson. Choose life. Celebrate life.

I took care of her as long and as well as I could. There were things I should have done better, but these I cannot now change. There were things I did well, and that was good. And now the hardest thing is saying goodbye. I do not know if she would understand or approve. Still, I will take my cue from her, and from what made her, once, everything to me.

Choose life. Celebrate life.

And so, my darling, I will do just that. It will dim the memories of us as I make new ones. The thought of that makes me sad and makes me miss you, but it must be this way.

I wish there had been a moment, a quiet time when you could have talked to me about this. I trusted you to know these things, to guide me when it all seemed black around me. And you always did, until . . . one day . . . you couldn't. And then you were gone.

It is too late to give you one last kiss. But I will live how you taught me and choose life and celebrate life, even though moving forward means leaving you behind.

Can there be, somewhere inside your mind, a way you can know that I will always love you? Always miss you?

I feel the touch of your hand in mine slipping away and then it is gone.

I will try not to be sad for what we once had and lost. That won't be easy in the dark of night when no one is looking and the tears still come.

Instead I will work to remember and to celebrate the wonder that we once were. I think that would make you smile.

It is time now. We must go different ways.

Dearest, dearest Jan . . . with you I once believed in forever.

And I believed I would never have to say . . . from Darling to Darling . . .

. . . Goodbye.

~*From Barry*~

I moved back to the United States in the fall of 2009, to begin living in Denver, CO, under a new contract arrangement with CBS News. It means time with my daughters and my granddaughter.

And it means a new beginning. In Denver, I am now with Mary Nell, that special someone I found despite all my doubts, and who has come to love me, whether I am a bad catch or not.

I am starting a new life with her, but one that also includes Jan.

I moved Jan from Bellevue, WA, to Denver, where she now lives in an assisted living facility. I visit her and oversee her care. It doesn't really matter to Jan since she often doesn't know me when I'm there. But, it matters to me.

Mary Nell encouraged me in this decision. She believes that she and I, and my daughters and granddaughter, and others who will come to know us, will help Jan by watching over her, and by spending time with her.

Some say it takes a village.

We are saying it takes a family, and now we will be one . . . for Jan.

Acknowledgments

THE PROS: Literary agent Paul Fedorko would not quit, while TV agents Richard Leibner and his wife, Carole Cooper, understood the importance of life "after," all of them from that magnificent firm NS Bienstock which has represented me for more than three decades.

Lynn Price at Behler Publications enhanced all she touched. Publicists Meryl Moss and Sarah Hausman of Media Muscle worked on my behalf from one end of America to the other.

THE READERS: I owe each for ideas freely shared. Nancy Jacobsen found a gaping hole and said fill it with a whole new chapter (I did) and my friend and colleague Jill Landes found a different chapter that didn't belong and said take the whole thing out (I did). Jill helped with national electronic media publicity and even roped her book club into reading an early version of "Jan's Story" for their insights.

Ideas also came from Gretchen Lobitz, Lynnetta Windsor, Brian Spano, Anne Drucker, Electa Anderson, a board member of the National Alzheimer's Association, my able assistant Kelly McDermott, and my cousin Marsha Tennant who wrote "Margaret, Pirate Queen" (Mirror Publishing).

JAN'S FAMILY: Caron Chorlton cares for her daughter to a depth only a mother can understand. She humbles me. Jan's aunt Ffolliott "Fluff" LeCoque is as flamboyant as her name. Her dance career started during World War Two and she continues working today. Yet, she always found time to see how I was coping.

In happier times, my brother, Erick H. Petersen, took the picture on the cover. John Carman usually photographs beautiful models and took a step backward taking a picture of the author.

Billie Tisch defines gracious and elegant. She was there, over and over, for Jan and for me. Her son, Andrew, took us into his family. His wife, Ann, once worked at WCCO-TV, where I also practiced journalism, but she did it better (I checked) and looks ever so much younger.

FRIENDS IN THE BUSINESS: Jane and Brian Williams first met Jan in Moscow and remember her as the wonderful woman she once was. Dan Rather dined with us in countries here and there, always gracious even as Jan was fading away.

CBS NEWS COLLEAGUES: When I asked her to write a foreword, Katie Couric immediately said yes and then talked with me about life and loss. Dr. Jon LaPook, the CBS News Medical Correspondent, wrote a blurb for the public and corrected my medical mistakes in private.

When I started at CBS News, Linda Mason was a producer in New York. She was relentless and exacting when she thought a script could be better. Today she is Senior Vice President for Standards and Special Projects and always wanted to know how was I, how was Jan?

Foreign Editor Ingrid Ciprian-Matthews would ask after Jan and then worry about me. CBS Weekend News Executive Producer Pat Shevlin was beyond patient. Paul Friedman, Executive Vice President CBS News, kept me focused on doing good journalism when my attention was pulled elsewhere, and thankfully so did Barbara Fedida-Brill, Vice President for Talent and Development.

CBS Evening News Executive Producer Rick Kaplan's had faith that I would deliver when I promised a story, and Senior Broadcast Producer Chris Dinan made damn sure I did.

Working with Charles Osgood of CBS Sunday Morning is always a privilege, and CBS Sunday Morning Executive Producer Rand Morrison is amazingly supportive of me.

CBS News and Sports President Sean McManus is a child, literally, of television. He is the son of James Kenneth McManus whom the world knew as the legendary sports broadcaster Jim McKay. Sean was exceedingly gracious when I needed to move back to America to start over again.

I owe every co-worker who got me through good days and bad, like Marcy McGinnis, Andy Clarke, Joe Halderman, Alec Sirken, Marsha Cooke, Mark Hooper, Lauren Wanko, Amiel Weisfogel, Steve Glauber, Jason Sacca. Correspondent Dan Raviv is a bestselling author of "Every Spy a Prince" who graciously brought my book to the attention of others. His wife, Dori Phaff, has been Jan's friend from the moment they met.

THE EXPERTS: Lisa Genova, author of "Still Alice," shared her journey openly. Her generosity overwhelms.

Meryl Comer cares for her husband with Alzheimer's at home and is President of the Geoffrey Beene Foundation Alzheimer's Initiative. She listens, understands, and encourages.

Dr. Marilyn Coors is Associate Professor at the Center for Bioethics and Humanities at the University of Colorado at Denver. Her thoughts forced me to have a few new ones of my own.

Dr. Janet Wessel Krejci, Dean of the Mennonite College of Nursing at Illinois State University, opened doors to Alzheimer's experts.

AND FINALLY: My fellow travelers made every gut wrenching moment of writing worthwhile. Let me share but one comment.

Edy Thogersen's husband, Al, is from the same Montana town of Sidney where I grew up. She was on the original Board of the McLaughlin Research Institute in Great Falls, MT, where they fight diseases like Alzheimer's, and she remains active in their fund raising.

She and Al live in a Continuing Care Retirement Community (CCRC). She sent this:

Barry,

I finished the book a couple of weeks ago and have struggled with words to describe its effect on me. Al has dementia but nothing dramatic like the anger you experienced from Jan. I have been lonely at times but that is one of the advantages of our living situation (in the CCRC). There are a lot of people here to share the misery.

Probably the most profound thing I found in the book was the change in your feelings of intimacy with Jan as your wife. It has taken me a long time to understand how different I feel toward Al and admit to myself that it is OK and a part of the process.

Thank you for being so open and forthright. It has helped me a great deal....Edy

To Edy, and anyone who finds help in this book, I thank you. I cried often in the struggle to get this story into words, but I kept going. You are the reason why.

RESOURCES PAGE

Start with the National Alzheimer's Association at www.alz.org

Its extensive listing of state and city Association affiliates is a doorway to finding support groups in your neighborhood. These are people already dealing with The Disease. One guaranteed surprise – you are doing a lot better than you realize.

The Alzheimer's Association shop at www.alz.org/shop and its partner products for sale at www.alz.org/partnerproducts offer DVDs, board games, and CDs with ideas for everything from creating shared memories with your loved one to explaining what is happening in the Alzheimer's brain.

Mark and Ellen Warner compile a daily Alzheimer's newsletter and run Ageless Design at http://www.agelessdesign.com When I moved Jan into Assisted Living I shopped at their on-line store for clocks, phones, and other practical items suited for the various stages of Alzheimer's.

CAREGIVING

Nobel Prize winning author Pearl S. Buck had it right when she wrote: "The person who tries to live alone will not succeed as a human being…His mind shrinks away if he hears only the echoes of his own thoughts and finds no other inspiration."

To see how you are doing with loneliness and stress go to www.alz.org/stresscheck/. If you think you can cope all by yourself, experts have a word for that…wrong.

The Well Spouse Association at www.wellspouse.org/ mission statement says: *"Well spouses help each other in ways no others, not even family, can understand."*

At www.caregiver.org, the website of the Family Caregiver Alliance, there are FAQs on caregiving, shared personal stories, a newsletter, and discussion groups.

At www.caregiver.com you will find topics like recipes for making meal times easier for caregivers. Here's a piece of advice they offer that I wish I could yell from the rooftop: "What about when friends and family ask, 'Is there anything I can do?' Answer -- Come for dinner Wednesday night and BRING DINNER."

At www.aarp.org/family/caregiving they address housing and mobility, grandparenting, life after loss, love and relationships, and have on-line communities.

The Rosalynn Carter Institute for Caregiving www.rosalynncarter.org/ was founded in 1987 at Georgia Southwestern State University in Americus, GA, honoring former first lady Rosalynn Carter. Their site's "Evidence Based Resources" section has podcasts and links like one to Medicare Caregiver Information at www.medicare.gov/Caregivers/ to help with navigating Medicare, and This Caring Home at www.thiscaringhome.org on how to make a home safe for those with Alzheimer's.

CLINICAL TRIALS

Clinical trials are happening all over the country. As an example, go to the University of California San Diego website at http://health.ucsd.edu/specialties/neuro/adrc/ Jan was evaluated for a clinical trial at the University of Washington http://depts.washington.edu/adrcweb/ There is also a national database of trials at: http://clinicaltrials.gov

NURSING HOMES AND ASSISTED LIVING

Try the American Association of Homes and Services for the Aging at www.aahsa.org, the Assisted Living Federation of America at www.alfa.org, the Consumer Consortium on Assisted Living at www.ccal.org, and the American Health Care Association at www.ahca.org

LIFE AND DYING

Don't ignore the legal issues surrounding this kind of diagnosis.
Update your will or trust. Get a Power of Attorney (POA) for
legal and medical concerns. As The Disease gets worse, more of
the decisions you once made together will be yours alone. Don't
screw this up, or you will be very, very sorry. One place to find
lawyers dealing with elder care issues is www.naela.org

Second, face the hard fact that the person you love has a terminal
illness. While she could still discuss these kinds of things, Jan
and I should have talked about how we wanted to be cared for
as life ends. We should have written our wishes down in a kind
of essay. Then I would have had her guidance. That would also
have given her family and friends a better understanding of
what I was doing and why. Resources abound at the National
Institutes of Health end of life site at
www.nlm.nih.gov/medlineplus/endoflifeissues.html

ONE LAST RESOURCE – YOU

A piece of advice earned with bitterness and tears: The Disease
twists and wrenches the brain. Prepare for having everything
organized and then be tossed aside by changes neither you, nor
all the experts, could predict. Be flexible and make your motto
these words from John Lennon:

"Life is what happens while you're busy making other plans."

Jan's Story
Discussion Questions

General

1. Why do you think Barry wrote this book, especially considering that he said he never intended to write it?

2. What did you learn about younger-onset Alzheimer's disease that you didn't know before?

3. Why do you think Barry calls Jan's diagnosis "The Disease" instead of Alzheimer's disease?

4. Barry made many difficult decisions during the course of Jan's disease. He predicts, "Some will take heart, some will condemn." Have you had to make any of these or other difficult decisions?

5. "Choose life. Celebrate life." Barry states that this is the most important lesson he learned from Jan during their many years together. How did Barry draw from Jan's wisdom in order to move forward with his life? What lessons have you learned from challenges in life?

Marriage

1. Barry unflinchingly describes how Alzheimer's disease affected his marriage, saying, "Being together was the core of our strength. The Disease attacked the core." How does Alzheimer's disease uniquely affect relationships between life partners?

2. Did it make sense to you that Barry deeply loves Jan yet found it more and more difficult to be around her as the disease progressed? Do you think it is possible to reconcile these feelings?

3. What thoughts and feelings did you experience when reading about the way Alzheimer's disease affected intimacy between Barry and Jan? Were you aware of this devastating consequence of the disease?

4. How did you feel about Barry's response to Jan when she offered intimacy to him one more time? How do you think you would have responded if it was your life partner?

5. What was your reaction to the suggestions of Barry's friends that he enter into a new relationship? How do you think you would cope with your feelings of guilt while making this decision?

Caregiving and Coping

1. Barry describes fear, anger, frustration, love, and loneliness as just some of the emotions he experienced as a caregiver. Could you identify with any of these feelings while reading about Barry and Jan's journey? Did you experience any emotions not mentioned in the book?

2. Uncertainty is identified as one of the worst aspects of Alzheimer's disease. Why do you think Barry says this? Do you agree, or do you think it would be more difficult to know exactly what was going to happen as the disease progressed?

3. How did you feel when you read about Barry's rage and how he dealt with it? Could you identify more with his rage or Jan's?

4. What signs of caregiver stress did Barry show over time, and how did he manage his stress? How would you have dealt with this stress? (For more information, see http://alz.org/stresscheck)

5. Were you surprised by Barry's early escape into "retail therapy" and his subsequent coping mechanisms? Do you engage in these or other coping mechanisms?

6. Barry said he did not realize he was slipping into a depression until it had reached a dangerous level. Were you alarmed by Barry's consideration of suicide? What did he cite as his reasons for not following through? Where might one turn for assistance in a similar situation? (For more information, see http://www.alz.org/we_can_help_24_7_helpline.asp)

Signs and Symptoms

1. Barry suggests that "Alzheimer's has immense patience." What does he mean by this? Do you feel this is a good or bad aspect of the disease?

2. When describing the years leading up to Jan's diagnosis, Barry asserts that "it was easy not to see it if you started out not wanting to see." Can you identify with Barry's denial of what was happening?

3. Jan experienced a difficult 3-day period just before her diagnosis. What signs did she show during this time? (For more information, see http://www.alz.org/10signs)

4. Barry provides clinical descriptions of the seven stages of Alzheimer's. How does Jan exhibit symptoms of these stages? Do the symptoms appear in an orderly fashion or do they manifest more chaotically?

5. What kinds of challenging behaviors did Jan display as the disease progressed? How did Barry and others respond to those behaviors? How have you handled these and other challenging behaviors? (For more information, see http://www.alz.org/living_with_alzheimers_behaviors.asp)

Support and Services

1.   What kinds of emotional and social support did Barry
     benefit from the most? What sources of support would
     you be able to draw upon in a similar situation? (For more
     information, see:
     http://www.alz.org/we_can_help_we_can_help.asp)

2.   How did Barry find Jan's live-in caregiver, Diane? If you
     needed this kind of assistance, how would you go about
     finding it? (For more information, see
     http://www.alz.org/carefinder/index.asp)

3.   Why did Barry move Jan into an assisted living facility?
     Do the same reasons apply to every family? What would
     be your benchmarks to indicate this kind of move was
     necessary?

4.   Were you surprised at the cost of long term care? How
     might you prepare for this kind of financial obligation?
     (For more information, see
     http://www.alz.org/living_with_alzheimers_financial_
     matters.asp)

This guide was prepared by the Alzheimer's Association
www.alz.org